BARRON'S PARENTING KEYS

KEYS TO TEACHING CHILDREN ABOUT GOD

Iris M. Yob, Ed.D.

D0068335

BARRON'S

Cover photo by Scott Barrow, Inc., Cold Spring, NY

DEDICATION
To Stephen and Elizabeth
Brent and Shane

© Copyright 1996 by Barron's Educational Series, Inc.

All inquiries should be addressed to:
Barron's Educational Series, Inc.
250 Wireless Boulevard
Hauppauge, New York 11788

Library of Congress Catalog Card No. 95-54008

International Standard Book No. 0-8120-9528-6

Library of Congress Cataloging-in-Publication Data
Yob, Iris M.
      Keys to teaching children about God / Iris M. Yob.
          p.   cm. — (Barron's parenting keys)
      Includes bibliographical references and index.
      ISBN 0-8120-9528-6
      1. Christian education—Home training. 2. Children—
Religious life. 3. Family—Religious life. I. Title. II. Series.
BV1590.Y63   1996
248.8′45—dc20   95-54008
                                     CIP

PRINTED IN THE UNITED STATES OF AMERICA
987654321

CONTENTS

INTRODUCTION

We live in an age that is noted for its greed, its crime, and its lack of values—at least on the surface. In reality, many people are looking for something more. They want peace of mind, a sense of hope and a feeling of purpose in their lives. Even more, they want these things for their children as well. They want to know how they can raise their children to live good lives.

Spiritual development is about learning values. It is coming to live reflectively. It is connecting with something or Someone greater than ourselves. It is having a growing sense that life has meaning from birth to death and beyond. It is regarding other living things on this planet with growing respect. It is learning to have faith.

Teaching about God is different from anything else you may share with your child. It means learning to live differently—to have hope and meaning, worthy commitments, and thoughtful decisions. In this sense, God is the name we give to whatever is most important in the universe. Yet this knowledge takes shape in the daily lives and ordinary activities of a family's time together.

The many faith traditions have their own understandings of God. While these differ in significant details, they also have things in common. This book is not written from the perspective of any particular faith. It looks at teaching about God in ways that will be helpful to people of all faiths and even to those who follow no particular tradition.

This is a book of ideas and suggestions. As you read it, some things will appeal to you; others will sound strange or even wrong to you. Choose whatever will serve your situation best and use the ideas here as jumping off points for further ideas and approaches to spiritual development.

The keys to teaching children about God are arranged in three parts. The first part addresses the questions a child sometimes asks—questions you may not know how to answer. How might you explain the big questions of life?

The second part examines the many ways children come to know God. You will discover that while your words are important, there are numerous other ways your child is learning faith—some you have planned for, some just happen. What can you use to teach her about God? How can you create the best environment for her spiritual development?

The third part looks at the wider context of learning about God. You will find out about the child as a learner and what other "teachers" the child might have. What do we know about the developmental stages your child is likely to pass through as he grows spiritually? How can your family relate to the world beyond the home to promote his spiritual growth?

Most important of all, the message of this book to parents is this: Do not be indifferent to your child's interest in God. This may be her best way to talk about the most important things in her life. It may be his best way of finding faith, hope, and meaning.

Part One

~~~~~~

QUESTIONS CHILDREN ASK ABOUT GOD

Often at the most unexpected moments, a child can surprise you with questions about God. Who is God? Where does God live? Who made God? Can God see me when I am in a dark cave? Can God do anything? How do I know God hears me? Why doesn't God fix things?

These kinds of questions and others make you suspect that children are born philosophers. They come into the world with curious minds that want to know about the meaning of everything they see in the world.

Although groups of believers usually agree on some things about the nature and reality of God, there is still a wide variety of interpretations among individuals and an even wider variety among different faith communities. Also, your own spiritual interpretations change and grow during a lifetime. The answers you give children will naturally start with your own ideas about God.

Among the difficulties you may face, however, is that you may not have found your own answers to these questions, or, if you have come to some understanding, you may wonder how you can put it into words that your child can understand. What can you say that makes sense to both of you?

This first part explores some of the richness of these questions and some guiding principles for parents who take these questions seriously. So, who or what, where and when, why and wherefore is God?

1

WHEN CHILDREN ASK QUESTIONS

No matter how difficult the question, there are responses you can give that make sense while opening the young questioner up to the mystery of God.

"Enquiring minds want to know"—so goes the slogan of a popular tabloid. In this at least they are right. Human beings reach out to the world with inquiries and questions. "What," "where," "how," and "why" are among the earliest words children learn. Every parent of a preschooler knows this only too well.

"Mommy, how big is God?"
"God is bigger than everything else. God is bigger than the world. God is bigger than the sky."
"Yes, but how big is God?"
"God is as big as the universe or bigger."
"Where does God live?"
"In heaven. Well, come to think of it, God actually lives everywhere."
"Why?"
"Because . . . Well, because God can see all the world and the stars and everything in the universe and take care of everything."
"Where is heaven?"
"Up in the sky."
"Can God fall down?"
"No."
"Why?"
"Because God is everywhere."

"Oh. Why?"
"Because that is what God is like."
"Why?"

Sooner or later you come to the question that baffles even you. Children can ask the most penetrating and unrelenting questions about all kinds of subjects, but when they get onto the topic of God, good and evil, or life and death, these questions can be the most challenging of all.

There are responses you can give that make sense while opening the young questioner up to the mystery of God.

Treat the Question Seriously By Finding the Appropriate Time To Answer It

Maybe your starting point is irritation. Here you are cooking dinner, and the dog needs to be fed, the table must be set, the phone is ringing, and you are asked, "How big is God?" Surely this is not an appropriate time to answer questions about the nature of the Divine.

The time might not be appropriate, but the question is. Right there and then, you can arrange a time by mutual agreement when the two of you can sit down and talk about the answer. Later that night, when the chores of the day are done and you are tucking your little one into bed, you might raise the question again and begin to share your thoughts and ideas about the possible answers.

Answer All Levels of the Question

Sometimes questions are more than a search for an intellectual answer. If the question was asked merely to get your attention or for some other reason not germane to the question itself, you will sense that, too. Nevertheless, by treating even these questions with seriousness and attention, no matter what might have prompted them, you are teaching your child that you respect and care about her—and that does not take you too far away from the right answer.

Be Truthful About Not Knowing All the Answers

You are not expected to know the answers to all the questions children ask. You may not be a philosopher or theologian. You may not feel you have all the right words. You may worry that you might give a wrong answer.

There may come a time, possibly when your child is becoming a young adult and less inclined to listen to your answers, that you will support him in taking his questions to a trusted minister or teacher. But you cannot and should not always defer to someone else.

You can find courage for this task by recalling what it means to teach about God. In the face of the infinite mystery that is God, your child is taking just her first faltering steps toward understanding. As a significant adult in her life, you have taken more steps on this journey, but the journey itself knows no end and lasts a lifetime. From this perspective, you are a learner, too. Some things you have discovered about God you can share, other things you still wonder about, and many things may always seem unanswerable.

By word and example, you can invite your child to join you on a pilgrimage of learning. Far better to admit that you do not know the answer, than always to feel compelled to give an answer that would limit God. Openness, honesty, questioning, and wonder are good habits. Someone who imagines she has all the answers will not have the joy of learning more.

With this in mind, you can say: "I don't know exactly how big God is, but I know that nothing in all the universe is bigger, stronger, or better. God is bigger than the sun. God is bigger than our house, or the tree you

4

climbed today, or the stars that are twinkling in the sky. And God loves us."

"But where does God live?"

"God lives everywhere?"

"Does God live in my room?"

"Yes."

"Does God live in the basement?"

"Yes."

"Does God live in my closet (my toy box, the refrigerator)?"

"Yes."

"How?"

"Nobody knows how."

"Why?"

"Because God is so special. But we do know God can be with us wherever we are."

When you do not feel that you must have all the answers, then you and your child can better sense the vastness and the wonder of the God you want to share. And the appeal of the divine mystery will take root and grow as together you earnestly ask your questions and search for answers.

2

~~~~~~

WHO IS GOD?

*There is no single or simple answer to the question
"Who is God?", so give the best answer you can to meet
your child's present interests.*

W hat can you say when your child asks you, "Who is
God?" This is not an easy question, especially when
you remember that the search for answers has occu-
pied—and baffled—philosophers, theologians, poets, artists,
and scientists throughout the centuries.

Today your child is likely to meet other children of very
different faiths—Jewish, Muslim, Christian, Hindu, Buddhist,
and others—along with children of no particular faith at all,
because our communities are becoming increasingly multicultural. Learning different ideas about God raises further
questions about who God really is.

For some native peoples, God is a striking natural phe-
nomenon. So when their children ask, "Who is God?", the
parents can point to a particular mountain, a river, an ancient
spreading tree, a huge stone, an animal like a bear or a lion,
or even the sun, moon, or stars.

For some, God is not personal but simply power—so
some Chinese talk about Tao, Indians about Rta, and
Iranians about Asha. For Hindus, the gods appear in many
forms. In Islamic, Jewish, and Christian thinking, however,
there is only *one* God, and this God cannot be seen, although
powerful and personal. Buddhism searches for the essence
of being, which is beyond God, so they do not speak of God

at all. For some, God is fierce; for others, God is indifferent; for still others, God is love.

Many of the words adults use to describe God do not always make sense to children. Theologians have given us words like *transcendent, omnipresent, omnipotent, sublime, supernatural, everlasting, ultimate, holy, almighty,* and *infinite*—words that we barely understand ourselves and that are more than hard to explain to young minds.

In giving answers to your child's questions, you can be guided by a simple principle: ***give the best answer you can to meet your child's present interests.*** To do this you might consider two things:

First, *what is his level of maturity?* This involves asking yourself:

- *What words can he understand?*
  - *Adults* might use the terms *eternal and infinite, transcendent, omnipotent, holy and ultimate,* and *just and merciful.*
  - *For a school-age child,* you might use instead *always and everywhere, above and beyond, powerful and almighty, awesome and perfect;*
  - *For a preschooler* you might use *always and forever and ever, high, strong, special and different,* and *good.*
- *What can you compare God with that is familiar to her?* We learn something new by comparing it with something we already know. So you might say something like:
  - "Let's think of the most powerful person you know. God is more powerful than him or her";
  - "God looks after us even better than mommy and daddy";

- "When I saw you being nice to that little child in the wheelchair, it made me think about God";
- "When the birds sing, they are telling us that God is looking after them."

• *What does she already know about God that you can build on?*

Even though the idea of God is big, we all start with our own perception and go on from there—no matter what age we might be. To answer the question "Who is God?" then, you may begin by first asking, "Who do *you* think God is?"

Second, *what is your child's particular need at the moment?* You might ask yourself:

- Is he asking the question because he's intrigued about the idea of God?
- Does she need reassurance that there is Somebody looking out for her?
- Does he need a sense of what is good to guide him in his moral choices?
- Has she just witnessed something inspiring that connects with the idea of God?

Having determined the context of the question, you can then formulate an answer that meets the level of maturity and the need that prompted the question in the first place.

In answering your child, your starting point may be a cluster of ideas that people of many faiths share. These ideas include:

• God is the *ultimate*. Nothing is greater. Through the centuries, people have died for their belief in God, so God was more important to them than life. To your child you might say, "God is the highest and the best in all the universe."
• God indicates *power*. That is why some say God has power to create, to destroy, to save, to demand obedience, to

8

overcome trouble, and to protect. You might say to your child, "God is the strongest and biggest in all the universe."

- God gives *meaning* to life. With God, the world we inhabit has both purpose and destiny, which explains everything. Even what seem to be chance occurrences fit into God's larger scheme. You might say to your child, "God has the answers to all our questions."
- God gives *hope*. By some means or other, when we have made a mess of things and evil seems to be winning, God provides a way out. Every faith identifies a way of starting over. You might say to your child, "God helps us deal with the evil that comes into our lives."
- God is *holy*. This puts God in a different dimension from everything else we know. God is respected and worshipped. You might say to your child, "God is special, in fact the most special in all the universe."
- Although God is ultimate, all-powerful, and holy, *we can know God*. Every faith in the history of the world has had its teachers and students. There have been prophets, scribes, gurus, monks, priests, preachers, and educators of every kind who have taught their people and their children about God. Parents who are asked questions about God find themselves thrust into this group of teachers. You might say to your child, "God is such a big idea, we will always find new things to say, but we can begin right now."

3

^^

WHERE DOES GOD LIVE?

Your child may need to see God in a particular place according to his present need.

The family was driving along late one summer afternoon. A storm had marched across the landscape earlier in the day and a few billowing clouds remained. As the sun was slipping below the western horizon, throwing its last light out across the sky, its rays fanned out through the patches between thunderheads, making the whole sky luminescent. Mom and dad were looking at the sky and commenting on the spectacle that stretched above and around them. From the back seat came a whispered question: "Is that where God lives?"

Children have a sense of home. Fortunate children have a sense of rootedness and safety, where all their things are, where they sleep at night, and where the family lives. Home for a child might be a neat suburban house, the combination of two or more places such as mom's place and dad's place, an inner city tenement, a sprawling country farm, or a shelter where they have just spent the night.

Whatever their picture of home might be, knowing where everybody lives helps to give order to the world by locating its parts in their proper places. A young child may want to know where airplanes sleep at night. Children wonder where the sun goes to bed. They like to find the homes of birds and squirrels and chipmunks. So quite naturally they wonder about where God lives.

We sometimes speak of the temple, church, or mosque as the house of God. Is this where God lives? your child may wonder. Do you want to restrict God to a particular sacred site? What about the other sacred buildings in town? Does God live in all of them? At the same time?

Two basic answers have been given to the question about where God lives. Some would say that God is above the world. This view emphasizes the holiness and transcendence of God.

Robert Coles, in his study *The Spiritual Lives of Children*, describes one boy's idea of where God lives. Andy was a ten year old who drew his picture of heaven. First he drew a wide rectangle. Inside of that was an oval shape that he filled with a variety of colors so that it looked like an Easter egg. This colorful place was heaven, he said, because it is pretty there. The building was gingerbread, he added, because it tastes good. The house was full of happy people. The background was black, because all the space between earth and heaven is black. In a small space in heaven, he drew the figure of a man. That was God, he explained, because God isn't alive the way we are and you can't really see God anyway.

By way of contrast, some talk in terms of God among us. They see God at work in the budding flowers, the flowing streams, and the moral choices people make. God is seen as close by each one of us, even within us. This view emphasizes the companionship and caring of God.

Coles watched as another ten year old, Morton, drew a steep mountain with a ladder reaching up to the top. At the bottom of the mountain were the Hebrews, clustered about the golden calf, representing their estrangement from God. On the pinnacle stood Moses with the tablets of stone on which were written the Ten Commandments. Above Moses was God's hand. Blue sky, yellow light, and red ties connected Moses and the Commandments and God, while all that was at the top of the mountain was connected with the people below by the ladder. Everything, in fact, was closely connected with everything else. Morton explained that God was angry about the people's disobedience and had to be soothed by Moses. Moses also became angry and had to be soothed by God. The things that went on at the bottom of the mountain had a visible impact on what happened above.

In this view, God is pictured as nearby, perhaps even like a family member or friend. With this in mind, we appreciate the life that we have, the world we live in, and those with whom we share it.

Most people who believe in God think of God as occupying any and all of the places mentioned here.

A starting point for dealing with questions about where God lives is to realize that *your child may need to see God in a particular place according to his present need.* These interests and needs vary widely but may include one of the following:

- *If he seems to be wondering about God's relationship to him*, you can talk to him about God being close by our side, listening to us, watching us, communicating to us through the things around us.
- *If she seems to be wondering about God's place in the wider universe*, you can talk to her about God being everywhere—by our side, in the world, and way out among the stars.

- *If he is wondering about where goodness or happiness comes from,* you may talk to him about God's home—Heaven or Paradise, for instance.
- *If she is wondering if God knows she is hurt, angry, or afraid,* you might assure her that God knows about her troubles and can help her deal with them.
- *If he has sensed the presence of God in a sacred place or at a special moment,* you might suggest that God was certainly there.
- *If she is wondering where she might see God one day,* you might talk to her about God being with us at the end of life.
- *Whatever may have prompted the question "Where is God?",* you can say, "God is everywhere. Where do you see God just now?"

4

CAN GOD SEE ME AND HEAR ME?

Ideas about God need to be personal.

Whether God is everywhere in the wide universe or pictured simply in heaven, your child may wonder what that means to her on a personal level. What difference does it make where God is? Can God see her? Can God hear her wherever she is? A number of things may prompt these kinds of questions.

Her own movements may make her wonder whether God can follow her. Children today probably move about more than at any other time in human history. Shopping trips, visiting family during the holidays, parents changing jobs, busing across town to school, and families splitting up and moving apart can take children away from their homes and into a new neighborhood, across the country, or even overseas. Does God keep up with them? they may wonder.

He may be experiencing a greater awareness of the size of the universe and may be having difficulty conceiving that God fills up all this space. A sense of space is one of the mental abilities children develop as they grow older. They increasingly organize themselves in terms of distances and directions. Up and down, near and far, above and below are among the earliest understandings. Then comes a sense of how near and how far—next door, on the next street, in the next town, county, state, country, on the next planet or star.

Ultimately, children come to the point where the immensity of space intrigues them and challenges them to imagine unbounded space. Increasingly, their appreciation of the location of God expands with their horizons.

She may be entering a space that is emotionally charged for her and wonder if she is entering it alone. From a child's point of view, going off to school at the beginning of the new school year, setting up home with either mom or dad in a new single-parent family, going to summer camp for the first time, or looking forward to an outing may seem like she is about to enter a new world.

This new space may be anticipated with fear and trepidation, excitement and a sense of adventure, or a mixture of feelings. Is she going to enter it alone? she may wonder.

He may have been involved in some mischief and may now wonder if God saw him do it. Mark knew that mom kept loose change in an old mug in the kitchen for the laundry and parking meters. The temptation to take a couple of dimes to buy candy proved too appealing. Later, he quietly panicked when he thought that although his mom might not know, Somebody did. God might even tell his mother.

A sense of the constant presence of God can be the beginning of a healthy conscience for children who are learning to respect both their parents' influence and their own ability to make choices. Or it can haunt and worry a child whose parents are controlling and authoritarian.

If God sees and hears them everywhere, then whether children see God there to help them do the right thing or to catch them doing the wrong thing so they can be punished depends to a large extent on how they view the presence of their parents.

15

Ideas about God Need to be Personal

This is especially so because we cannot see or hear God but believe God sees and hears us wherever we are. Here are some exercises that you might like to consider. They are arranged in order to suit children of varying ages, starting with the youngest.

• Share with your child a picture of a large landscape—a playground, an underwater scene, a countryside, a fair, and so on—especially one that shows lots of people and activities. Have him locate in the picture all the places he would like to be and would not like to be. Have him talk about the "good" places and the "horrible" places. Then ask him if God is in each of the places that were pointed out—for instance, Is God here in the clouds? on top of the ferris wheel? in the dark woods? as high as the sun? with the children swimming in the water?

• Play a game you can call "Make a Sound." Have your child make as loud or as soft a sound as possible—by voice, or drum, or hand clapping, for instance. Ask "Who might be able to hear it?"—the person on TV (the loudest noise cannot be heard); the neighbors; the person in the next room; the cat sleeping; you with your eyes closed; your child with his eyes closed; God (no sound is too quiet).

• Look at some objects through a magnifying glass, telescope, binoculars, or 3-D microscope. Talk about God's eyes seeing all these things.

• Have your child draw a picture of "God hearing" or "God seeing."

• Together make a list of things God can see or hear. Depending on the age group, you might include:
  – God *hears* prayers, cries, breaths, songs, heartbeats, ants' footsteps, stars moving, plants growing, and thoughts;

16

– God *sees* every grain of sand, the bottom of the ocean, the far side of the moon, inside a bee's head, the whole of the sun, inside the darkest cave, every word in every book that has ever been written, and secret motives.

In each case, explain that these powers of God make God special, they are good things and they mean God can help us wherever we are.

5

WHERE DID I COME FROM?

The question about where everything began may be best answered with a story.

E very parent, it seems, is one day asked, "Where did I come from?" Sometimes children are indicating they want to know where babies come from. In that case, you would offer lessons on sexuality, mothers and fathers, families and love, and the responsibilities and opportunities of being male and female.

On another occasion, given the mobility of our society, children may simply want to know what part of the country or the world they came from. Where were they born? How different or similar are they to their friends and neighbors?

Significantly, there are also times when the question is much more far-reaching. Where did they come from in the very beginning of everything?

Jennifer was sitting with her dad looking through the family photo album.

"This is Jennifer," says Dad, "when you were just a new baby. And this is Mommy, and here is Daddy holding you in your new blanket."

They turn back a page or two. "This is our wedding picture. See, Mommy has a lovely bride's dress. And look, there is Grandma and Grandpa. They are Mommy's mom and dad."

"Oh yes, and Gramps and Gran."

18

"They are Daddy's mom and dad."

Silence ensues while this information is processed. Then Jennifer asks, "Who is Grandma's mommy and daddy?"

"Look, here we have a picture of them. See, they are standing here by their old car. It was a new car then, and we all used to go for a picnic in it."

"Who are their mommy and daddy?"

Dad sees where this questioning is leading, but answers on. "I don't have their photo. They lived a long time ago."

"Who was their mommy and daddy? Who was the mommy and daddy way back in the beginning?"

Through the ages, human beings have wondered about where everything began. One of the traditional arguments for the existence of God goes something like this. What causes the grass to grow? The rain. What causes the rain? The clouds. What causes the clouds? The sun's warmth heating the water on the surface of the earth. What causes the water on the surface on the earth? The rain. But what caused the first rain? God did. In other words, so the argument goes, something or Someone must have started everything going.

The world we live in is full of wonders and our children are full of questions. Why is the sky blue? Who taught the animals to hop and jump and run and fly? Who makes the sun move across the sky? Who changes day into night? Who built the mountains or dug the canyons? Who makes the plants grow? Where do babies come from? Where did it all begin?

The stories of beginnings that most religions tell and the stories that the sciences tell do not always agree. Many people have found a way to reconcile the two that sufficiently satisfies them. Many others do not like to think about it at all because there doesn't seem to be a single good choice. Still others reject one view altogether and hold fast to the other.

There is a way of sharing a sense of God in the beginning without engaging in this debate. Whatever particular understandings about the origin of the world you may come to, *you can enrich your child's understanding of where she came from by telling the stories that the various faith traditions have offered.*

That is because the creation stories give more than just facts. They speak about meanings, values, and relationships—the relationships between humankind and the other creatures we share this planet with, between one human being and another, and between humanity and God. From the religious stories we can learn more about what life is and how it should be lived.

Keep in mind these significant points when telling stories:

- *Stories speak to us on a number of levels* and the story of God creating the world is no exception. Some approach these stories as literally true, others take them to be figuratively true. In either case, the power of the story lies in conveying the idea that our origins, and therefore our lives, have meaning.
- *Do not belabor the point*—let the story do the telling.
- *Tell the story to make a particular point for your child's benefit.* It may be that she need never feel alone; Somebody thought she was needed in the world; she is worth something; everything else she shares the planet with is also important and has its own place and purpose.
- *Tell the story of the world's beginning in a way that brings delight and answers.* The question about the meaning of life will take a simple form for children:
  - The youngest child may simply want to know why giraffes have long necks, why zebras have stripes, and why birds have wings.

– A child a little older may wonder more about what place human beings were given in the world.
– An even older child may focus his questions on the relationship between males and females, between human beings and the natural world, or between humanity and God.

So adapt the story to address the appropriate age level and the kinds of questions asked. Knowing that God was there in the beginning, a child can grow up with healthy, strong ideas about who he is and how he should relate to others. If he gains a sense that there was a reason for his life, he will find greater purpose and meaning in living.

6

WHERE DID GOD COME FROM?

The timelessness of God is a good introduction to the act of faith.

Most parents know that tracing the human family back to the first beings or God's acts of creation does not satisfy a child in the long run. There is still an unanswered question. Where did God come from? God made everything, but then, who made God?

Just as a child wonders about where God came from, he may be just as curious about where God is going to end. Grandpa died and Mom explained that he was an old man and was tired and sick. What about God, then? Isn't God old? Will God, too, disappear?

The usual answer to the first question is that nobody made God. We say God was always there; there never was a time before God; God goes back forever and ever; or God was the beginning and there was nothing before God. And just as faith has envisaged God at the beginning of everything, so it also sees God at the end. God is older than everything else in the whole universe but will never grow old, because God lives forever.

Even in reminding yourself of these answers, you know they simply do not make sense in a world that does not know such permanence. Everything in human experience has a beginning and an ending. How can something always be there from before the beginning and last until after the end? No one knows. So how can you explain an everlasting God to your child?

Your best approach may be to steer away from answering endless questions about how God can be eternal, and use *the timelessness of God as an introduction to the act of faith.* Faith is different from other kinds of knowing.

By faith, we accept some things about God as true, even though we can never explain how they are so or prove that they are so. Lacking a reasonable explanation or clear evidence, however, does not make the claim about the eternal nature of God untrue. We know it to be true because the scriptures, the prophets, our tradition, or our teachers have said it is so and we trust them. When a question has been pursued as far as you are able, but the answer is not satisfying, you may have to say, "I don't know any better answer than that. I just know it to be so."

A trusting faith is not a bad thing. We all trust some things to keep life going. Believing in an eternal God is not stupid, irrelevant, or harmful. Such a belief can have great meaning and significance in the believer's life. Your challenge is to help your child have faith in what is good and appropriate.

Considering the maturity level of the child and the specific needs he might have at the time, you might find one of the following approaches helpful in explaining what faith is.

- You might illustrate faith by *reminding your child of other things we have faith in*—especially those drawn from her own experience:
  - You know that when you walk out the door in the morning you won't fall off the earth.

23

- You know that the medicine you take will make you better, even though you don't know how it works.
- You do as your parents tell you to do, even when you sometimes wonder why, because you trust them.

- You can *tell a story of faith.* Every tradition has such stories of people who believed, trusted, and acted on their beliefs even when it seemed unreasonable or risky to do so.

- You can *expose your child to the mysteries that surround the nature of God and the limits of human understanding.* An older child especially will delight in exploring the puzzle of God through riddles such as this one from Chinese Taoism:

> When we are dreaming we do not know we are dreaming. Only when we wake up do we know we are dreaming. Sometimes we even have a dream within a dream. We can dream we have woken up and know we were dreaming in our dream. Only in the ultimate awakening shall we know that this life and all that we think we know is nothing more than an ultimate dream. Yet fools think they are awake—so confident that they know they are princes or herdsmen or something else! You are a dream and I who call you a dream am also a dream.

- You can *be a model of faith* for your child. You show your faith in God despite the mystery of divinity by your
  - *eagerness to go on learning about God.* For instance, does your child see you reading, thinking, and talking about these things as though they were important to you?
  - *humility in talking about God.* For instance, have you found the ability to be sure without being dogmatic? to know what you believe without condemning others who believe differently?

Today's world is characterized by more change than most other periods throughout human history. Everything seems to be in flux. In this setting, God can be the one thing that is constant and unchanging, even though you cannot always say exactly what God is or why you accept the idea of God at all. Yet faith that God was there in the beginning and will be there in the end gives life purpose and gives the future hope. The attempt to teach your children faith in an everlasting God, then, is well worth the effort.

7

WWWWWWWWWWWWWWWWWWWWWWWWWWWWWWWWWWWWWWWWWWWWWWW

WHAT HAPPENS WHEN I DIE?

In preparing your child to live with the knowledge of death, show that life in all its stages can be celebrated with God.

One of the sad realities of life is that nothing lasts forever. Flowers die and leaves fall from the trees. Tabby the cat and Peppy the dog will die and children see their death and mourn. Sometimes they lose grandma or grandpa, mom or dad, even a brother or sister. Children lose playmates to guns, accidents, and disease. And sometimes they face their own death through illness or accident.

It was once thought that children should be protected from acquaintance with death, but a realistic look at what a child experiences today, through television and newspapers and in the schoolyard, suggests that you cannot shield him for long from such knowledge. Since dying is as much a part of the human experience as being born, protecting your child from knowing about death is misleading and does not prepare him well for what inevitably lies ahead.

Unfortunately, much of what a child learns about death is unrealistic. Cartoon characters are killed many times over but keep coming back to life again. Bodies accumulated in electronic games are tallied gleefully. Deaths on television are too numerous, too remote, and too momentary to give a child a full sense of the loss they really stand for. Some children live in places where death is so random and frequent that they expect to die as much as they expect to live to adulthood.

The idea of the God who has no end plays an important role in explaining all endings—including our own—to your child. During different times and in different places, people have held various views on the meaning of God's endlessness. The common hope is that although everything on earth dies, God brings about new beginnings. Most views agree that God has a plan for human beings that lasts forever, just as God, too, lasts forever. This idea suggests that it is important to live a good life now. It also assures people that ultimately good will win over evil, justice will be done in the universe, and all wrongs will be made right.

In preparing your child to live with the knowledge of death, show that life in all its stages can be celebrated with God. Whether your child is facing the prospect of her own death or the loss of a loved family member, consider these activities.

- Retell the stories about what comes after death *from your tradition* and, where it seems appropriate, those *from other faiths as well*. In this Muslim story, for instance, the joy of one day meeting God is powerfully expressed:

     The blessed have entered Paradise and are enjoying all its beauties and pleasures. One day, an angel comes from Allah and stands on one of the great walls surrounding Paradise. He calls out to the people in a magnificent voice.
     "There is a promise yet to be fulfilled. Your greatest happiness is to come."
     Dressed in their richest garments and royal crowns, the people mount the finest horses and set out from their homes in procession through Paradise.
     They come eventually to a wide open space, where a great gate is opened for them, a gate as wide as east is

from west in earth measurements. They pass through this gate into an enormous valley, where the soil is made of finest musk and saffron, its pebbles of gold, its trees branching low with luscious fruits, its flowers blossoming in splendor. On bejewelled, satin-covered seats beneath the trees, the people take their place.

The finest meal in their entire experience is served them—foods that had never tasted so good. Drink is poured for them into goblets of pearl and jacinth.

All of these things are as nothing compared with what is about to happen. Veils of light, which protected them from the overwhelming sight of Allah, are raised and they look upon God without harm or injury. They fall down and in deep humility say: "Glory be to Thee, O our Lord. In Thy praise Thou art blessed and exalted and blessed is Thy name."

- *Plant a memorial garden or tree.* When there has been a loss, a living thing is a positive symbol of the everlasting and sustaining power of God. This growing thing shows rebirth and the continuity of life.
- *Make a family tree.* Record not only the names and dates of as many family members as you can (with photographs, where possible), but also include a brief statement of something noteworthy about them. It may be as simple as "Came to this country from Japan in 1926" or as exciting as "Joined a wagon train to Colorado," or as interesting as "Made the star pattern quilt on the wall." Make sure the child's place is marked on the family tree.
- *Write a tribute* to a family member recently lost. It can be a record of special memories, funny things that happened, favorite sayings of theirs, or what the child liked about them the most. Put the tribute in a special place for remembrance.
- *Join in a formal ritual or develop one of your own* to mourn a death and celebrate a life. Like many other religious traditions, the Greek Orthodox faith has a recurring ritual called *Mnemosino* or *Remembering.* Forty days

after the funeral and then on a yearly basis, the life and death of the loved one is remembered in a simple ceremony. The family prepares a tray of grains spread out in a pattern, over which sweets or candles are arranged in the form of a cross. After readings and prayers at the church, the grains and sweets are spooned into small sacks and presented to each of the guests. As they take the gift, they respond, "God forgive him (or her)," thus putting the past to rest in the mercy of God.

- *Show that while we can be glad for a life, we are sad about a death.* Do not shield your child from the grief, outrage, or sadness that is appropriate for deaths on a large scale as a result of war or famine, the lonely death of a homeless person, the agonizing death of a cancer patient, the tragic loss of life in accidents, or the loss of a family member. Assure her that God sees and knows the loss, too.

8

~~~~~~

WHO IS THE STRONGEST IN THE WHOLE WORLD?

You can share with your child moments of wonder and thankfulness where you see the powerful hand of God at work.

A s children make sense of their world, they want to find their place in it and know that that place is safe. They want to know who is the strongest person at school—they or their best friends or the teachers or the bullies in the higher grades. Could their dad beat up so-and-so's dad? Who has the best car? Whose house is the biggest? Who has the latest and best toys? Who has the biggest guns, the best airplanes, or the fastest ships? They may want to know, Who is the strongest person in all the world?

At first glance, these kinds of questions may strike us as self-centered. In fact, they may indicate that a child is feeling vulnerable or powerless. With such feelings, confidence may fade and his world may become a place of fear. Realizing that he is not the strongest person in all the world, he naturally figures he might gain strength by associating with whoever is the strongest. With dad on his side, or the teacher, or big sister . . . or God, he can face anything!

Gerardus van der Leeuw, a scholar in world religions, came to the conclusion that the idea of power underlies most beliefs about God. Whatever people might call this power, they see it in the natural world around them—in the changing seasons, the movement of stars and sun, the uncanny abilities of animals and birds and fish to survive. They see it in their own lives—in birth, growth, and death, and in love, courage, and wisdom. And they wonder how they can connect with this power.

Van der Leeuw tells a story to illustrate this. He learned from his investigations that an ancient African who is about to embark on an important expedition might step on a stone. He feels the impact of the stone on his foot and recognizes that here is something powerful. He picks it up and says to it: "Ha! Are you there?" His belief (and hope) is that the power of the gods is in the stone. He pockets it for his journey in the faith that it will make his expedition successful.

Of course, faith today usually takes a different form from this, but still there is a strong belief that having a relationship with God means connection with power. That is why many people pray in the morning that the power of God will protect and sustain them through the day. They pray for the sick, the troubled, and those in danger. They pray for success at the beginning of a new venture, and they thank God for giving them the strength to complete a task. They pray to overcome evil and do the right thing.

You know the dangers and difficulties of growing up in today's world. How can your child be protected from violence—even when it is offered to her as entertainment? How can she resist the temptations of illicit drugs and irresponsible sex? How can she be saved from despair and hopelessness in a world that seems at times to be consumed with materialism, crime, and hate? How can you give her faith, hope, and love? These questions can prompt you to look for help beyond yourselves, perhaps in the power of God.

31

Some find evidence of the power of God in miracles, and most traditions tell stories of miracles. Just as significant are the moral choices and changed lives that God empowers. Accounts are told of ancient prophets, reformers, and modern leaders who have stood for truth or just causes and sometimes persuaded a nation to do the same because they were connected with God. Belief in God has strengthened Christians through persecution brought against them, Jewish faithfuls through pogroms inflicted on them, and Muslims through jihads they have waged to protect their faith. The idea that God made all people equal empowered the message and life of Martin Luther King, Jr.

Although miracles are spectacular and stories of changed lives are inspiring, they are not the only times we see the power of God. God often works in quiet ways. The daily renewal of energy, the birth of a baby, daffodils in spring, and luscious fruits in the fall are witnesses to the forces put in place by God.

You can share with your child moments of wonder and thankfulness where you see the powerful hand of God at work. There are a number of forms this sharing might take:

- *by reacting positively* to stories and accounts of miracles and courageous choices made by others;
- *by recounting events* in your own lives in which God's power was revealed;
- *by accompanying your child* on mountain trails, beach strolls, bird-watching, star searching, garden tours, and wherever you can witness the quiet sustaining power of God;
- *by thanking God* for supplying your needs;

- *by facing the crises* in your family life with calm assurance and trust, while also being honest enough to admit your fears, anxieties, and doubts;
- *by chatting* with your child about the possibilities and challenges of life, perhaps around the dinner table, on a drive in the car, or at bedtime.

As you send your little one out into the world each day, you cannot always know what he will encounter, nor can you protect him from every danger that might cross his path. You cannot answer every question asked of him, or decide in every case what he will participate in or what he will reject.

To teach your child about a God who is powerful is to give him courage and security. The idea of God might be like the stone an African carries in his pocket making the journey through life successful.

9

DOES GOD GIVE ME
WHATEVER I ASK FOR?

You can teach your children that God does more for us than give us everything we might want by teaching them how to ask.

You like to give your child what she wants. You wish for her to be happy. You like to see her face light up when her expectations are met. You plan her holiday presents and are willing to go without things for yourself to make sure she has what her heart is set on. Giving your child good things is one of the ways you show your love for her.

The downside of this picture is that children can be overindulged. In the shopping malls and toy stores, in advertisements and by word of mouth, children learn early what it is that they want. In many homes, children's rooms and toy boxes overflow with board games, dolls, cars, books, brand-name sneakers, cute outfits, wall decorations, computer games, and electronic toys.

In this context, it might be helpful to look at the word *spirituality*. Spirituality is a difficult word to define. It has to do with looking beyond surface appearances to deeper meanings. It means cultivating the values of the human spirit as God intended—values such as wonder, appreciation, peace, joy, and caring for others.

We can understand spirituality better if we understand what it is not. Probably the most accurate opposite of spirituality is materialism. Materialism is the accumulation of things especially when they are valued above everything else. This is one of the greatest temptations of the western world. We have more money to buy more things today than other cultures and times have known.

Wise parents are judicious about meeting their child's every demand. They distinguish between wants and needs. They unstintingly fill the *needs* their child has for love, companionship, security, predictability, firmness, nourishment, and trust first.

They also address the *wants* a child might express, but they know that what a child might want is not always good for her. Wants seem to have no end—the more she has, the more she can think of that she wants to have. Adults as well as children know this to be true.

Wise parents are careful not to encourage their child to be selfish or greedy. They know that there is more to happiness than collecting lots of stuff, having the most or the best things, or being the first to have the latest "in" thing. They want their child to put the right value on money and family resources and to think of the needs of others. They know that sometimes going *without* can help a child value more what she already has.

If parents can be wise in providing for the needs and wants of children, God will be even wiser. It is often said that all the resources of the universe are at God's disposal. Because God sees the end from the beginning, God knows what we most need and how to meet that need. Besides that, you will probably tell your child that God hears her when she asks for what she *needs*. When a child puts all this together in her mind, she can gain the impression that God is like Santa Claus—simply there to give her whatever her heart desires.

What can you do to help your child see a bigger picture of God? *You can teach your child that God does more for us than give us everything we might want, by teaching her how to ask.*

- *Ask for others as well as for herself.*

  One of the antidotes to selfish thinking is to remember the needs of others. A child will know someone who is sick, unhappy, angry, or in trouble. She will have seen people in distress on the TV news and in the newspapers. In the light of others' needs, her own wants are put in better perspective and her requests to God are likely to reflect wider concerns.

- *Ask for good things.*

  A little self-evaluation can be very helpful here. Before prayer time, you might ask: "What shall we pray about tonight?" As various items are mentioned, you can talk about their importance, what difference they can make, who will be made happier (or unhappier) if this request is granted, and so on. This way, you can lead your child toward making appropriate requests.

- *Thank God for all the good things already given.*

  Sometimes you can play the game: "Tonight I am glad for . . ." Each family member in turn says what it is in the day that was wonderful for them. You can teach a child to be thankful even for things that at first glance didn't seem so good—the rain that spoiled his picnic made the farmers' crops grow; the day spent in bed sick gave him a chance to listen to the birds sing; when his friends were unkind he had the courage to be nice to them, and so on. By focusing on what God has already given, your child can learn to be more content and less demanding.

- *Be thankful even when the answer is "no."*

  When a child is disappointed that God did not give her what she asked for, you can talk to her about the importance of "no" answers. By way of illustration, you might remind her of times when you have said "no" and why you did that. You can tell her that God sometimes says "no" because God is wise and knows what is best for each person.

10

xxxxxxxxxxxxxxxxxxxxxxxxxxxxxxxxxxxxxxxxxxxxxxxxxxxxxxxxxxxxxxxxxxxxxxx

WHY DOESN'T GOD DO SOMETHING?

Big disappointments in life should be treated with honesty and positive action.

Alex was just ten when his mother was diagnosed with terminal cancer. He agonized through the chemotherapy and radiation treatments. He heard his mother's cries and groans. Through it all, he prayed for God to save her. He watched as she grew progressively weaker, eventually lapsing into unconsciousness and dying. After the funeral, he declared he hated God.

In a very real way, Alex experienced what is perhaps the most significant test of faith. How is it that God is powerful and caring yet seems to do nothing to prevent suffering? Why doesn't God do something to make the pain stop, to prevent bad people from hurting others, to bring the rain to drought-stricken farmers or to bring war to an end? There are a host of occasions of human extremity when the intervening power of God seems needed, but nothing happens even though earnest people have prayed.

Dealing with disappointment or disaster in the experience of children demands a great deal of gentle wisdom and patient understanding on the part of parents—a demand that is often made all the more difficult because the parents may be sharing in the disappointment or tragedy. In these circumstances, **big disappointments in life should be treated with honesty and positive action.**

38

Treating Disappointments with Honesty

Encourage Your Child to Tell You How He Feels

As Alex watched his mother slowly die, he experienced a range of feelings, which he later acknowledged. He felt grief, frustration, possibly fear for his own life and well-being, guilt over times when he was not the perfect son, and he even hoped at one point that his mother *would* pass away so that they could resume their normal lives again. Keeping these feelings to himself would have left Alex alone to deal with them and, just as important, to sort out his thinking about God. Having somebody to talk with, however, can give him support and courage to deal with these emotions in healthy ways.

If your child has been accustomed to finding you a good listener, one who will always meet his openness not with judgmental responses but with understanding and care, then he will more likely make you a confidant in his crises. Listen patiently, allowing him the time to work his way toward a healthy resolution. Sometimes this process cannot be hurried or preempted by giving him the "right" answer immediately. At first, your advice may be less helpful than your patience and understanding. Eventually, you may offer some positive alternatives to the way he is thinking.

Give Your Child Other Means of Expression

Many children in trauma cannot express their inner thoughts and feelings in words, but they may be able to do so through drawings, movement, mime, or music. They may be able to talk with you about their feelings more easily after they have expressed them in another medium, although some may not be able to speak of them at all.

You might ask your child to show you where God is in her drawing or music or other expression. Do not overreact if her picture does not agree with what you believe it should. As time passes, you can suggest other more positive images.

Share Your Own Fears, Anxieties, and Doubts

Spiritual life is often compared with a journey or pilgrimage. None of us has arrived at the final destination—we do not have all the answers to life's dilemmas. You can show your child that you, too, have doubts and questions as you endeavor to remain true to your beliefs. By your example, you can show him that questions are not wrong and searching for answers may take some time.

Treating Disappointments with Positive Action

Put Suffering in Proper Perspective

Every faith tradition gives an account of suffering in human life. Buddha saw it as evidence that life as it is often lived is skewed and out of balance, like wheels whose axles are off center or bones that are dislocated in their sockets. In our experience, evil seems random and inexplicable. In an important sense, it is God's enemy, too.

To put suffering in proper perspective, begin by explaining that if God gives life and happiness, then evil comes from somewhere else. In part, human choices bring trouble to people's lives. Some accept the existence of an evil force. Most faith traditions have stories to tell about the rise of evil in the world. So God is not to blame when things go wrong.

All faiths, however, do more than simply describe suffering and its effects. They look beyond to a better time when death, suffering, and evil are finally overcome. Show your child by story, picture, or sacred text that God is with us during hard times and has something better in store. In the perspective of the future, suffering is temporary and relief is coming.

Help Your Child to Find a Positive Action She Can Take to Address the Disappointment

You can do a number of things with your child, some more public than others, such as:

- Participate in a fund drive for medical research as your contribution to overcoming a disease;
- Make a patch for a quilt or a whole collage to commemorate the good things you recall;
- Design and illustrate a poster of encouraging texts to be displayed in the child's room;
- Compose a true account or a poem about the experience to be shared with others;
- Write out a promise to live healthfully or stay away from guns or drugs and display it prominently.

By all these means, you can lead a child into healthy ways of dealing with difficulties in his life that leave his faith and belief in God intact.

41

11

WWWWWWWWWWWWWWWWWWWWWWWWWWWWWWWWWWWWWWWWWWWWWWW

WHAT DOES GOD LOOK LIKE?

Show that all the children of the world are part of God's family.

Margot tells how she decided to take Lisa, her granddaughter, to see the Christmas decorations. Their tour ended downtown, which was trimmed with colored lights, Christmas trees, and lighted candles. In one spot was a nativity scene set up by one of the local Christian churches. They gathered around the scene, pointing out Mary and Joseph, the wise men and shepherds, the sheep, and of course, baby Jesus.

Looking at the doll that represented Jesus, Lisa asked, "Is that a girl doll or a boy doll?"

"A boy doll," responded Margot. "Jesus was a baby boy."

"Oh, then," replied Lisa, "we must go and get a girl doll, too."

Despite the apparent facts of the Christian story, Lisa, at three years of age, did not want to be left out of the picture in an event that was so central to her faith.

Many children have the idea that God is an elderly white male with a beard and slightly balding. Theologians, however, usually agree that God is a spirit, neither male nor female, because God is not human. Pictures we might have in our mind of what God looks like are simply our ways of visualizing God so that we can relate to God.

People are much more aware today of the racial, ethnic, class, and gender mixes of their religious communities and their neighborhoods. They may be surprised sometimes to discover how limited their views are of the human family and of God and how excluded some might feel from their faith.

Groups of people tend to view God as one most like themselves—whether they are Asian, African, Caucasian, Middle Eastern, or Pacific Islander—while they have at the same time understood that God is above all and for all.

There is no single or simple way to reconcile this tension between culture and religious belief, but it is a situation you may have to deal with. You may want to consider:

how inclusive your view of God is and to what extent it welcomes different peoples;

whether your view of God can or should be enlarged;

how God can be presented in a broad enough way to encompass everyone.

Whatever your particular beliefs might be, however, most parents would want to *show that all the children of the world are part of God's family.* On the basis of this underlying principle, the following approaches may be useful.

Retell the Stories and Laws That Show God Reaching Beyond Gender or Ethnic Boundaries

Many religious faiths offer important instruction on how to treat strangers or anybody who is different. A believer's duties might include hospitality, protection, honest dealings, and sharing his faith with others. The writings of Isaiah in the Bible announce that God's house is to be a house of prayer for all peoples. The Bible's New Testament gives accounts of Jesus' relationships with others who were usually excluded from public gatherings—lepers, tax collectors, poor people, Samaritans, and known sinners. The racial equality espoused

43

by Islam has attracted many ethnic minorities. If the faithful are to regard others with respect and care, then their God certainly does also.

Use Inclusive Language

Words are important in our understanding of God. If you want your concept of God to be wide enough to include the whole world of children, you need to use broad words to describe both God and the world.

For instance, compare the sentence on the left with the one on the right in each of the following pairs. Notice how much more inclusive the right-hand sentence is in each case:

God made *mankind*.	→	God made *humanity* (or *humankind*).
Man should obey God.	→	*Human beings* (or *people*) should obey God.
A child can give *his* heart to God.	→	A child can give *his or her* heart to God.
		or *Children* can give *their* hearts to God.
We are the *sons* of God.	→	We are the *children* of God.
God cares for all *his* children.	→	God cares for *all* children.

Look for translations of sacred texts and story books that use inclusive language while remaining true to the writer's intention.

Offer an Imaginative Picture of God That is Inclusive

In a model village set up by New Zealand Maoris in Rotorua, there has been a conscious effort to claim God for the Maori people. Sitting in the chapel overlooking a lake, one can see the water through a large glass door behind the pulpit. Etched into the glass is a picture of Jesus walking on the water, according to the Bible's Gospel story. He is shown dressed in Middle-Eastern garb with sandaled feet. For all intents and purposes, this is a traditional depiction, except that the Christ figure is in fact Maori, with the facial features and decorative markings of the Native New Zealander.

God is considered by many to be one but with multiple sides, depending on different perspectives. Chief among the Hindu gods are Vishnu, Shiva, and Brahma, three male gods, but many also accept the goddess Mahadevi as the mother of all.

A number of artists are experimenting with a Christa figure rather than a Christ figure. A crucifixion scene will show a female on the cross. Of course, on a literal level, the Jesus of Christian belief was a white male. On a figurative level, however, these artistic representations may be attempting to show how accessible God is to all, despite differences among us.

Figurative representations using various and even non-traditional symbols may be more appropriate for an older child. You can lead her into an appreciation of the meaning of the artwork by asking her: "How is this picture different from our usual picture?" "What does this picture teach us?"

Part Two

▲▲▲

HOW CHILDREN LEARN ABOUT GOD

S o far, we have talked in general terms about answering children's questions about God. Beyond answering their questions, however, what specifically can be done to teach your child about God? What resources do you have? What means for teaching are there that you can use in the home, at worship services, and in the world around you that will provide you and your child with an exciting and revealing understanding of who God is?

This section explores the many different sources at hand that you can use—sources that have been developed and used by faith communities for centuries. Again, not all resources will be appropriate to all faith traditions, so select those that best represent both your tradition and your child's interests.

12

~~~~~~

UNPLANNED LEARNING

A child's total experience of the good, the true, and the beautiful teaches her about God.

T he home is the child's first school in matters of faith and spiritual development, and parents are the child's first teachers. The lessons learned at home are often more lasting and more meaningful than those gained in any other setting.

Children's learning takes place on two different levels, because parents teach their children in two different ways. There is the learning that goes on all the time, as children watch and listen and interpret what they see and hear around them—even when you are off guard. This is unplanned learning. It is happening even though you have not deliberately planned for it or even intended for it to happen. This is the power of your example at work.

Then there are occasions when you deliberately teach, using all the resources at your disposal, adopting strategies that you hope will be effective and keeping specific objectives in mind. This is planned teaching.

Planned teaching can only be as effective and persuasive as the unplanned learning it builds on. A common thread must run between what we do and what we say, between what we live and what we teach. When our living and our teaching are in harmony with each other, our teaching can be very effective.

Because learning occurs anywhere and all the time, you should endeavor to create a whole environment that teaches your child about God. In a real and positive way, *a child's total experience of the good, the true, and the beautiful teaches her about God*. These qualities can fill your home and lives because they are as much a habit of being and a way of seeing as they are a fixed reality.

The *good* is a big idea. It includes outward rule keeping and inward intentions to do what is right. It means not only avoiding what is wrong, but also doing what is right. It incorporates being fair, kind, caring, respectful of others, generous to the needy, patient, and loving.

The *true* is an equally big idea. It invites us to consider whether we really are what we pretend to be. It means that our words and deeds can be trusted and our dealings are honest. It is about keeping promises, avoiding malicious gossip, and telling the truth even though it might hurt us. It suggests the search for knowledge that is right and uplifting.

The *beautiful* is an idea that goes far beyond how things look on the surface. It means being attractive in who we are, not just in what we look like. It means finding something that satisfies the soul in the long run and not just pleases for the moment. It suggests finding the lovely all around us in what we see, hear, taste, smell, and touch. It invites us to do our part to add to the beauty in our world and to treasure and protect what beauty there is.

The following questions will provoke your thinking about the goodness, truth, and beauty in the home you share with your child.

48

- *Do you notice the good, the true, and the beautiful?*
Two things can make us blind and deaf to the good things around us. One is noticing only the bad; the other is not noticing anything at all!
  - Do you notice when winter turns to spring; when flocks of birds circle to prepare for migrating; when your floor needs sweeping; when your child needs to have his hair cut or to learn table manners?
  - Do you know how your child spends his leisure time?
  - Do you notice when your child comes into the room?
  - Do you make time for your child during the busy day?
  - Do you speak well of others when they are not there?
  - Do you affirm or thank your child more often than you correct her?
  - Do you share with your child your enjoyment of a new flower, a starry sky, a bird's nest?
  - Does your child know what you value?
- *Do you surround yourself with the good, the true, and the beautiful?*
The good, the true, and the beautiful come in many shapes and sizes. More often than not, they do not depend on large amounts of money, but they may require effort and some wise choices.
  - Are you happy with the choice of magazines that come into your home?
  - Do the TV shows you or your children watch represent the spiritual values you believe in?
  - Is your home and its surroundings neat and clean, orderly and calm, and thoughtfully decorated?
  - Is the music you listen to uplifting, honorable, and enjoyable?
  - Does your family enjoy leisure activities together that build spiritual lives?
  - Do mom and dad speak respectfully to each other and to the children?

- Do you practice forgiveness toward each other without holding a grudge?
- Do you have the habit of really listening when a family member is talking to you?
- Do you smile and laugh with your child?
- Does your child know you trust him and that you can be trusted?
- Are your business dealings honest and helpful to everyone involved?
- Do you tell your child that you love him?

• *Are you growing toward the good, true, and beautiful?*
Spiritual life is a way of growing, often likened to a journey. Sometimes the way is smooth, sometimes it is rough, but overall it has a destination—we journey toward God. That means we increasingly understand and reach toward goodness, truth, and beauty.

- Do you care for your own physical, mental, and spiritual needs as well as those of your child?
- Do you take time to reflect on your life to find healing and hope?
- Do you think about priorities in your life and from time to time adjust your activities to meet those goals that are important in the long run?
- Are you grateful for the life God has given you and are you determined to live it fully and richly?
- Do you think about the good, the true, and the beautiful that is all around you?

13

~~~~~~

PLANNED TEACHING

In planning to teach, consider when you shall teach, what you shall teach, and how you shall teach.

Although you may be actively involved in a faith tradition, there are times when you will need to plan for teaching to supplement what your child may pick through personal appreciation and understanding of that faith just from growing up with it. On some occasions you will want to set about in a deliberate way to make some lessons clear. In planning for these occasions, ask yourself these questions: **When shall I teach? What shall I teach? How shall I teach?** This key addresses each of these questions in turn.

When Shall I Teach?

- *Choose a regular time.*
  In the hustle of everyday life, the best intentions can be lost under the pressure of other commitments. A good safeguard is to assign your teaching a regular time slot that becomes part of the daily routine.
- *Choose a time that can be special for both you and your child.*
  You can arrange it so that time spent learning about God is different in quality from time spent doing most of the other things our daily lives demand of us. It is a time for growing faith and exercising imagination so it should be an unhurried and quiet time. Sandwiched in between the

end of school and swimming lessons may not be as good a choice as at the end of breakfast before the school bus arrives (providing you and the family are up early enough to have the time for this) or as a bedtime ritual before the light is turned off.

• *Make it a quality time rather than a long time.*
Although teaching a child about God is one of the most important things you will ever do for him, the teaching need not be drawn out. A regular, special time each day that is filled with wonder and insight, although brief, will have a greater impact on his life than long and tedious occasions. It is better for him to leave the time looking forward to tomorrow's encounter than to be restless and bored. You might experiment with these time allotments (but be willing to adjust them to suit individual attention spans):

  – 3–5 minutes with *infants*;
  – 5–8 minutes with *preschoolers*;
  – 5–10 minutes with *elementary school ages*;
  – 3–10 minutes with *adolescents.*

What Shall I Teach?

• *Various faith traditions are treasuries of spiritual truths.*
Insights into the nature of God and the meaning and purpose of life have been collected and preserved within the various faith traditions. These insights come in a variety of forms that suit different ages. For instance, you might find with your child that

  – simple stories, action songs, and memorizing verses are appropriate for *preschoolers*;
  – action stories, songs, memory verses, and simple doctrines are best for *five to eight year olds*;
  – hero stories, straightforward poems, learning about traditional rituals, doctrines, and moral choices are good for *nine to twelve year olds*;

       – religious histories, literature, the music and art of
your own and other religions, biographies of spiritual
leaders and novels that explore questions about Who
am I? and What should I do? are helpful for *teenagers*.

• *Make use of published resources.*

Many religious groups offer prepared materials, often in
daily lesson format, that make your task so much easier.
Look for materials that deal with significant faith issues,
are attractive to look at, and offer the kinds of activities
that appeal to your child.

How Shall I Teach?

• *Use a variety of teaching approaches.*

Among the possibilities at your disposal are story telling,
asking questions, explaining in your own words, reading
out loud, singing, praying, sitting quietly as you watch
something as stirring as a waterfall or a magnificent painting, or talking over the events of the day.

• *Use a variety of teaching aids.*

When you realize that children learn about God through
all their senses, you know you have many resources to call
on when you teach. There are the scriptures of the various
faiths—some of which are published as children's edi-
tions. There are historic stories and parables—many
appearing as children's literature. There are workbooks,
catechisms, and home lesson guides for teaching major
religious beliefs. There are noble men and women whose
exemplary stories can be found in biographies and autobiographies. There is the natural world in the parks, wood-
lands, oceans, open fields, and close at home in the garden
and along the street. Your pets are a part of nature that has
made a home with you. There is music and dance on your
cassette player, TV, and in concert halls and on stage that
you may find uplifting. Your child may be able to play or
compose music. There are sacred places and sacred times

around town and in your own home. There are your conversations with your child and the questions you ask each other to help her think about what is important.

- *Encourage a variety of learning responses.*

Sometimes good teaching consists of you giving answers; sometimes it consists of you evoking and encouraging responses from your child. The old adage, "We learn by doing," is true. If your child is going to "do" something to "learn," however, even that must be planned for. You may need to

- suggest an activity (a drawing, a story, a reading program);
- supply materials (play dough, a library card and regular visits to the library, dress-up costumes, writing materials);
- pose the right kind of question to get him thinking about an answer;
- provide a quiet work space.

14

^^^

LEARNING BY
ALL MEANS

*Build up a child's understanding of God in many
ways and through many viewpoints.*

As already noted, God is not available to us directly
through sight, sound, touch, smell, or taste. In fact, no
scientific probe or procedure has been able to expose
God to us or even to prove that God exists. Through the
faithful imagination, however, we do develop a picture—or
more accurately, a number of pictures—of God that help us
penetrate divine mystery and come to know God.

The word *picture* as used here is to be broadly understood. It is not intended to mean only what might appear as
paint on a canvas. There are also other kinds of visual pictures as well as sound pictures, pictures in movement, word
pictures, and so on. Some may prefer to call them concepts,
perspectives, or views.

Different faiths offer different kinds of pictures. In the
Jewish faith, there is a prohibition against "graven images,"
so sculpture, painting, and drawing have not been significant
ways of communicating concepts of God. Muslim and some
Christian denominations have been particularly strong in
designing a sacred place for worship. The cool, clean floors
and reflecting pools within mosques point to God as a resting
place in a dry, dusty land, and the single, stunning spire

reminds the worshipper of the oneness of God. Protestant Christians at the time of the Reformation whitewashed church walls to cover the ornate art work and broke many religious statues as a declaration of their different view of God. For them, music and preaching came to play a greater role. In some traditions, worship services are ritualized, while for others, a preacher's words are central. Buddhist and Hindu sacred places are characterized by many beautiful statues.

No matter what "language" or medium is employed, a person can spend a lifetime coming to know God better. So, within the boundaries and strengths of your own faith, ***build up your child's understanding of God in many ways and through many viewpoints.*** Whether the knowledge you develop with your child comes from music, architecture, sculpture, painting, dance, scripture, or natural wonders, these principles may help guide you in their use.

Share Different Views of God You Can Find in Your Faith Tradition

You may be quite surprised to discover how many different portrayals of God there are even within your own scriptures and sacred places, let alone among various traditions. Some of these concepts will emerge in stories, particularly those that recount how people encountered God and what they saw or imagined. Some will appear in poetic, descriptive, or historical passages in scriptures. Some stories are passed on by word of mouth. As you share these with your child, encourage her to recreate the portrayal in her own mind and share with you what it suggests to her about God.

Develop Different Kinds of Pictures or Concepts of God from Your Faith Tradition

Even though a faith tradition may be strong in a particular medium (be it architecture, music, visual arts, meditative techniques, written text, theology and preaching, or ritual), most will also have some supplemental ways of picturing God. Use as many different "languages" or media as your tradition permits. Especially, look for those kinds of pictures that match the learning style of your child. Some children learn well in sound, others in sight, and still others in movement. By sharing concepts of God in many different ways, the composite picture will take on greater depth and meaning.

Explore the Multidimensional Impact of Knowing about God

Understanding God as, say, King, Mother, Creator, or Life Force will affect your child on a number of levels. It will have an *intellectual* appeal. That is to say, it will suggest how God relates to human beings and what God is like. It will also have an *emotional* appeal, for the picture will arouse its own kind of response, whether of awe, attraction, thankfulness, or worship. It may also have a *moral* appeal because it may suggest how we should behave in the presence of God. So as you talk with your child, be prepared for these various effects.

Let Several Different Images or Concepts Work Together

Older children and adolescents in particular can be challenged when they see that some pictures do not fit together with others very neatly or consistently. For instance, in Jewish writings, God is portrayed as both a lion and a lamb. The writers of the four Christian Gospels each developed a different picture of Jesus: Matthew described Jesus as king; Mark spoke of him as a servant; Luke presented him as the ideal man; John portrayed him as the Son of God. Hindus speak of God in three major forms: Brahma the Creator, Shiva the Destroyer, and Vishnu the Preserver.

Each of the conflicting views is believed to be correct although conceptually different from the others. It is not always possible to resolve these conflicting perspectives—it becomes a matter not of either/or but of both/and. As young people compare and contrast these pictures, they gain a better sense of both the inadequacy of human understanding and the depth of meaning in the idea of God.

Allow the Images and Knowledge of God to Grow and Change

Words and other "language" used to portray God are suggestive. Their richness can be explored from many different perspectives. In exploring images of God, encourage a sure approach rather than a dogmatic one; a learning stance rather than an opinionated one; a willingness to learn more rather than a sense that one knows it all already. Then your child will sense that his pilgrimage is underway and that there will always be more to know.

The keys that follow examine specific ways of teaching using various faiths' "languages."

15

~~~~~~

LEARNING THROUGH SACRED WRITINGS

Bring scripture alive for your child's ongoing spiritual development.

Most faith traditions have a collection of sacred writings. For Jews, there is the *Torah*; for Christians, the *Bible*; for Muslims, the *Koran*; for Hindus, the *Baghavad Gita*; for Buddhists, the *Tripitaka*; for Jains, the *Agamas*; for Confucians, the *Five K'ing*; for Taoists, the *Tao Te Ching*; and so on. These books, usually considered the word of God, are a treasury of literature on spirituality and faith.

These writings—sometimes the collections of many authors, sometimes a collection of several books from the same author, sometimes the single writing of one inspired individual—have been preserved and revered through generations of believers.

Different faiths approach their sacred writings differently. Jews and Christians intellectually wrestle with their scriptures to understand them and to pass on their understanding to their children. By contrast, for many Indians, the *Veda* holds a special place as sacred writing but its contents are not always well known to believers. Just memorizing the words even without understanding them is considered a significant religious duty.

Whenever the *Koran* is quoted, a Muslim will repeat a formula similar to: "He—Elevated is He—says. . ." Because the Koran is considered the most sublime word of God, only the "purified" may touch it or recite it. Muslims want to recite its words as beautifully as they can, so young children with the most promising voices are sent to the mosque to memorize it and learn how to chant it melodically. It is wrapped in stunning materials and placed at the highest level in the mosque, often suspended from the roof or set on the top shelf.

A difficulty you may encounter in sharing scripture with your child is that sacred writings are not easy to read or understand. Their language is often old fashioned, their meanings obscure, and their ideas difficult for young minds to comprehend. They have been the study of scholars throughout time who admit that they have not uncovered all the truths they contain. In the Muslim tradition, for instance, there is one claim that an early mystic had seven thousand interpretations for every verse of the Koran.

Despite the difficulties, scripture is an important source for learning about God. ***Bring scripture alive for your child's ongoing spiritual development.*** These strategies may help you open these treasures to your child.

Explore the Variety within Sacred Writings

Most sacred writings are made up of a variety of literary types: poetry and song, story, doctrine, moral codes, and descriptive passages. Although children should eventually be acquainted with all this variety, specific kinds of writing appeal to children at different ages. As a general rule, you might use:

• *for preschoolers*:
  – straightforward stories, especially those involving children and animals;

60

- simple explanations of right and wrong;
- songs or poems with some repetitive phrases or sentences.
- *for early elementary school ages*:
  - action stories;
  - descriptions of direct encounters with God, both positive and negative;
  - moral rudiments, such as the Ten Commandments;
  - songs or poems with a story line or literal plot.
- *for later elementary school ages*:
  - stories of role models;
  - simple doctrinal passages that outline key beliefs;
  - occasions that represent moral decisions and religious duties;
  - songs, poems, and prose to be memorized.
- *for adolescents*:
  - stories that mark significant moments in the development of a religious community;
  - deeper study of key beliefs;
  - moral codes and the meaning and origin of significant rituals;
  - songs and poems that are increasingly symbolic.
- *for young adults*:
  - accounts of historical eras;
  - theological and philosophical issues to do with faith;
  - key understandings of other religious traditions;
  - principles of interpersonal relationships and relationships with God;
  - epic stories and symbolic writings.

Present Scripture in Ways that are Interesting to a Child

Most sacred writings are written by adults for adults. Although it is well to acquaint your child with them in their original form, you may also consider some additional ways of presenting them:

- read from children's versions if these are available;
- retell the scripture in your own words or in words that your child can understand;
- use songs, actions, videos, audiocassettes, picture books, activity books, story telling, and other children's activities to introduce the scripture to her.

Help Your Child to Memorize Significant Passages

Children between the ages of three and ten are able to memorize more than they can understand—in fact, their ability to memorize is quite phenomenal. This fund of memorized material can remain with them and be recalled at important moments in their later lives, when they can understand and appreciate it even more.

In learning passages of scripture by heart:

- Adjust the length of the passage to the age and attention span of the child—from a sentence for infants, to longer passages for young children (when the ability to memorize is at its height and the sense of achievement can be sustained), to verses and paragraphs for older children;
- Use as many avenues as possible for becoming acquainted with the passage to be memorized—that is, have the child simultaneously say it out loud as he is reading it and listening to you read it;
- Use songs, actions, and rhymes as prompts in recall;
- In general, repeat the whole passage rather than break it down into individual words and sentences, because the words and sentences can be recalled more easily as strings of associations and connections.
- Make an exception to this rule when memorizing lists of ideas or things. In committing to memory the Ten Commandments, for instance, it is easier to memorize ten key words (one for each commandment)—"have," "make," "take," "remember," "honor," "kill," "commit," "steal,"

"bear," "covet"—than to remember the whole Decalogue in order.

- All these memory activities will be counterproductive, however, if the task is made a burden. Let your child feel the success of the undertaking by encouraging and commending her efforts along the way.

16

∿∿∿

LEARNING THROUGH SACRED HISTORIES

Stories about the past have a great deal to say about the present and the future.

Within many sacred writings and other materials, faith traditions pass on a knowledge of their history from generation to generation.

Such sacred histories serve important purposes. ***They have a great deal to say about the present and the future.***

- *They shape a sense of spiritual identity* because they answer the questions "Who am I?" and "Where did I come from?" They detail the nature of the relationship between the individual and God.
- *They help establish a sense of community.* Sharing an historical understanding strengthens the bonds among people, giving them a sense of their place in the stream of time and a common language and symbols on which to build faith.
- Many of the stories recall the deeds of people from the past who can *serve as role models* for new members of the community. In both their successes and failures, they can provide an honest picture of spiritual life.
- Retelling encounters with God from the past *can assure a community about the future.* If God has led, guided, instructed, and prospered a people once, then they can face tomorrow with greater confidence.

Inherited sacred histories may very well differ from the histories being written today. They may be made up of accounts of real events as they were remembered and recorded, but they may also contain stories that are known to be legendary or mythical. But both factual and imaginative stories that have been preserved for the benefit of a community of believers contain important spiritual truths. Some of these truths and insights are communicated literally, others figuratively, and together they build faith and a knowledge of God.

Humanize the Stories

History does not have to be a dull recitation of facts. Rather, it is made up of real people doing real things with real feelings. When Moses climbed Mt. Sinai to talk with God, his heart was racing; when Peter walked on the water to meet Jesus, his bravado was obvious; when Buddha sat under the Bo tree, he was exhausted and discouraged, but then became restful and calm and finally deeply joyful and excited. Emphasizing the people in these stories will make your sacred history more memorable and more relevant.

This is true even for known mythical accounts. The gods and the legendary heroes of religious imagination can also be presented with feelings, motives, intentions, and responses. Often the most significant truths from fictional accounts are truths about the human predicament and human hope. So tell these stories with the same fullness and richness as those that are known to be factually true.

A simple aid to telling stories is for the story teller to visualize the setting and action in her own mind. Then in describing what she sees, hears, smells, touches, and feels, she will tell a story that is lively and vivid.

Connect the Historical Events with the Present

There are many ways to bring history into the present. You could ask your child to imagine a moment in his own life that resembles the story in some way. For an older child, you might have him speculate about how the community's life today might be different had a different decision been taken or had a different sequence of events unfolded at some significant historical point.

For children of all ages, you can begin to connect current ritual practices with their origins. For instance, you might explain why particular candles are lit at special moments, why certain foods are eaten, why particular ceremonies are performed, why gifts are given on occasions, why services are held at appointed times, and so on. If they are old enough, they might be taught the ritual along with the history and begin to participate in it within their families and communities.

Another way of connecting history with the present is to encourage an immediate response from the child after she has learned the history. This can be in the form of a play reenactment of the story, with the child and maybe also the parent and other family members taking the roles of different characters in the action, if you can arrange this. You could also encourage your child to draw a picture or make a model of what she imagined the action to have looked like; or she may write about her response. You might like to give her the starting phrase, such as: "When I hear this story about [whatever], I feel . . ."

Present the History in Ways Applicable to the Age of the Child

Very young children do not fully understand the measurement of time. They may not even be able to string a simple sequence of events together logically. For children up to about the age of seven, then, the important things to be learned from the sweep of the past are the major events.

As children grow older, cause and effect and a sense of what followed what become increasingly interesting and significant.

For adolescents, time lines and a sense of the passage of various eras helps them to locate themselves and events of the past more precisely.

17

LEARNING THROUGH PARABLES AND OTHER STORIES

Explain the unknown by talking about the known.

A parable is an earthly story with a heavenly meaning. Parables and many other illustrations point beyond the events they talk about to a greater truth. They obey the maxim of good teaching: ***Explain the unknown by talking about the known.***

For example, here is a parable drawn from Hindu literature. It explains the difficult concept of reincarnation.

The king asks Bhanto Nagasena, the elder, "Does rebirth happen without the person 'passing over,' as it were?"

"Yes, Your Majesty. Rebirth takes place without anything passing over."

"How, Bhanto Nagasena, does rebirth take place without anything passing over? Give an illustration."

"Suppose, Your Majesty, someone were to light a light from another light. Has the first light passed over to the second light or is it still there?"

"It has not passed over."

"In exactly the same way, Your Majesty, does rebirth take place without anything passing over."

"Give me another illustration."

"Do you remember, Your Majesty, when you were a boy and learned a poem from your poetry teacher?"

"Yes, Bhanto."

"Pray, Your Majesty, did the poem pass to you from your teacher?"

"No, truly, Bhanto."

"In exactly the same way, Your Majesty, does rebirth take place without anything passing over."

"Bhanto Nagasena," said the king, "then what is it that is born into the next existence?"

"Your Majesty," said the elder, "it is name and form that is born into the next existence."

The parables of lighting a candle from another and the memorizing of a poem from teacher to student made teaching this mysterious concept much easier.

Locate the Parables and Stories from Your Faith Tradition

Every tradition is rich in such parables and illustrations. Add to these the sacred histories, biographies, significant events, and stories that can often be understood as parables as well, and the number will surprise you.

In Jewish and Christian scripture, this story is told:

Jonah, a reluctant prophet, was sent by God on a mission of warning to the Assyrian capital of Nineveh. In his trepidation and doubt, however, Jonah fled in the opposite direction to Tarshish. On the way, a terrible storm threatened the ship in which he was traveling. The sailors figured that the storm was sent as a punishment and were determined to find who on board was guilty. The lot fell on Jonah, who was thrown overboard, and the storm abated. Jonah, however, was not lost, for God also sent a big fish, which swallowed him.

For three days he was captive in the fish's belly until he was spewed up on the beach near Nineveh. Understanding that the hand of God was at work in the storm, the fish, and the rescue, Jonah went into the city and preached his message of warning as God had first asked of him. His preaching was amazingly effective, and the Ninevites, long time enemies of Jonah's people, repented and God saved them from impending disaster.

Jonah found this difficult to accept given the hostility they had shown the Jews. He sat discouraged and disappointed above the city waiting for the threatened destruction to come, but it did not.

This well-known story has a number of important lessons. It demonstrates that the Hebrew God was to be seen as god for all peoples, Jews and non-Jews. It also illustrates how even a chosen one, a prophet in this case, may misunderstand the nature and actions of God. It suggests that people should examine their lives and motives to be sure they are doing God's will.

Invent Parables of Your Own
As you teach, you will often have occasion to reach for an analogy that best illustrates your meaning. Do not hesitate to have your child share in this creative endeavor with you. You might ask her:

"What is God like?"

"How do you think of God when you see the sunset? the sunrise? a storm? a landscape? a baby? . . ."

"What is life like?"

"How is goodness different from evil?"

Explore the Meaning of the Parable or Illustration
At times, the meaning is obvious as soon as the illustration is given and needs no further comment. At other times you might like to delve into an illustration for a deeper appreciation of its meaning.

For a younger child, you can explore the illustration that goodness is like day and evil is like night, for instance, with guiding questions like these:

What do you see (hear) in the day? at night?
Where do you like to be in the day? at night?

What do you like to do in the day? at night?
How do you feel in the day? at night?
What is the difference between day and night?

For an older child or young person, your guiding questions might not only search an illustration's meaning but also expand its reach.

In exploring the question What is God like?, Annette replied, "A painting."
"About what?"
"It's an amalgamation of all the pictures of Jesus I have ever seen."
"Where is this picture?"
"I see it hanging on my bedroom wall."
"Does it change or is it always the same?"
"God's always the same."
"What does this picture do for you?"
"It's my whole life. I would never want to think about it not being there."
"What is the face like?"
"It has blue eyes. And they are not looking at me."
"Where are they looking?"
"Inside of me. There doesn't seem to be physical contact, and yet I know there are eyes because I feel them as well as see them."
"Do you see only a face or is there more?"
"I see the part that is intelligence. It doesn't matter if there are hands or the shape of a body, but there is . . . I don't know. There is just a being."

And so the discussion continued, touching sometimes on what was visualized and at other times on what it might mean. Such expansion and exploration of an illustration of God can make God more real.

71

18

~~~~~~

LEARNING THROUGH DOCTRINES

The fundamental beliefs of a faith tradition have meaning when they are related to a child's life.

Most faith traditions have developed a set of fundamental beliefs. These fundamental beliefs or doctrines usually address in a formal way the basic questions of faith: Who is God? What is human nature? What is the relationship between God and humanity? Where did everything come from? Where is everything going? What is good? How is evil dealt with?

Teaching doctrines, however, can be one of the most challenging tasks for parents because children often find this kind of learning tedious and quite boring. Part of the lack of interest is due to the abstract nature and language of doctrinal claims and part is due to their lack of connection with the child's everyday life.

To make the learning of doctrines both interesting and appealing to young minds, ***relate these fundamental beliefs to the life of your child.*** This can be done in a number of ways.

Lay a Foundation of Implicit Concepts at an Early Age
    The formal beliefs of a religious group do not exist in a vacuum but are distilled from the stories, histories, parables, hymns, poems, and expositions of faith that the tradition has

collected and preserved over time. Interpretations and formal statements of beliefs are implied in these collections. Learning the doctrines, then, becomes a logical step taken after children have become well acquainted with these collections.

Avoid Formal Doctrines Until Your Child Can Properly Deal with Them

Doctrines are usually given in abstract, systematic, formal language. This becomes abundantly clear when you look at examples of doctrinal statements, in this case all dealing with a similar understanding about living a good life:

> "I have hidden your word in my heart that I might not sin against You." (Jewish)
>
> "Christ dwells in the regenerate heart, writing upon it the principles of God's law, leading the believer to delight to obey its precepts, and imparting power for such obedience." (Christian)
>
> "He who performs actions without attachment, resigning them to God, is untainted by their effects as the lotus leaf by water." (Hindu)
>
> "God guides us in the straight path, the path of those on whom God hast poured forth grace." (Muslim)

In these examples, notice the following:

> abstract nouns are used: for example, *principles, obedience, attachment, grace*;
>
> difficult concepts are named: for example, *word, sin, regenerate heart, imparting power, resigning . . . to God, poured forth grace*;
>
> complex images are used: for example, *hid in my heart, Christ dwells in the regenerate heart, God guides us in the straight path, resigning them to God*;

73

each statement makes sense as it relies on other statements in the whole system of beliefs: who God is,
what God's law is, what God's power is, how human
beings are connected to God, and so on.

If your child is seven or eight years old or younger, she
will probably be thinking in concrete, random, and informal
ways. She will usually have little appreciation of doctrines,
beyond a surface recognition of certain words. For her,
restate beliefs in simple words: for example, "God will help
you do the right thing."

If your child is older, especially about to enter adolescence and the teen years, he is more likely to understand and
even enjoy the finesse of words and meanings, the logic of
the system, and the organization of ideas.

Relate Doctrines to the Experience of Learners

Use a situation in the life of the young learner as a point
of entry into a doctrine. In the above examples, for instance,
you could begin with a discussion of the difficult position a
young person is in when his group of friends is about to
embark on some wrongdoing. He does not want to lose their
friendship and acceptance within the group, but neither does
he want to be involved in their planned activity. What does
God want him to do? Where can he go to get help? How can
he get this help? The answers to these questions lead into the
doctrine.

In relating experience with the systematic formulations
of beliefs of a faith tradition, you can make connections on a
number of levels. At the *intellectual* level, you will call on
reasoning and logic, memory and imagination. Together, you
can think your way through the situation toward the belief
statement. At the *emotional* level, you will call on feelings,
attitudes, hopes, and desires. Here you both will be honest
about what he wants now and in the long term, how he feels

about the alternatives, and what might motivate him to choose God's way.

The intellectual and emotional levels are important in making a real connection with all the doctrines. A personal, inner response along with an intellectual assent makes any doctrine more real, more valuable, and more enduring. Ask your young person how she feels when she understands who God is, or what God requires of her, or who she is as a follower of God, and so on. This personal involvement with the beliefs of a faith tradition is the best antidote to tedium and boredom.

Move from Illustrations and Examples to the Doctrine
If doctrines are the distillation of knowledge drawn from the collected stories, histories, parables, poems, and hymns of a tradition, then a young person should be able to follow this same logical route.

This strategy may be helpful. Lay out before your child a number of texts or stories that illustrate a similar truth. Together, look for the commonalities and differences among them. Prompt and guide him through this process with questions that encourage him to think in broad terms. Typical questions would be: What did God do the same in each of these stories? What do these meetings between God and human beings tell us about ourselves? What makes the difference between good action and evil action?

19

‸‸

LEARNING THROUGH PEOPLE

Learning about the spiritual life can be nurtured by learning about the spiritual lives of others.

In studies of how children learn, researchers confirm what most parents know intuitively: Children are great imitators. They learn some of the most difficult things simply by copying what they see others do.

Take learning to speak for example If you've tried to learn a foreign language, you know how complex a task it is to speak with the correct words, grammar, phrasing, idioms, and accent. Yet long before she goes to school, and without anybody deliberately giving her lessons, your child learned to speak her mother tongue. It seems she learned to do this simply by listening to others speaking.

She learns a lot of other things this way too, as any parent of a toddler soon discovers—how to treat others, how to get what she wants, what to do with various implements, and how to get dressed.

As a child grows, hero worship increasingly becomes a molding influence in his life. He dresses, walks, talks, and adopts the attitudes of those who are his heroes. To your dismay sometimes, these role models are not always who you would choose. In a way, your child is acting out through his idol his growing independence from you, a stage that is not necessarily unhealthy, despite your anxieties.

Be encouraged that even if the models you have held up for him are now apparently rejected, when a child's life has been filled with strong positive examples, these influences will linger and often outlast these stages of self-assertiveness.

During these years, in less obvious ways than for a younger child, you may still find opportunities for putting her in touch with spiritual exemplars to compete with the stars of rock, film, and sport that are part of her world. The books, movies, people, and places to visit that you have some control over can be chosen with spiritual objectives in mind.

Rarely do we find anything more powerful than teaching by example. And this is true in learning about faith as well. In the lives of people who have been on a spiritual quest, all the abstract questions and beliefs become concrete, all the high-sounding truths are put to practical use, the rules for moral conduct are acted out as good or bad behavior, and belief and trust in God are put to the test. In fact, *one of the most effective ways of learning about the spiritual life is by learning about the spiritual lives of others.*

Here are some things to consider in providing your child with spiritual models.

- *Examples abound of people who have led rich spiritual lives with all their ups and downs:*
  - the founders of religions—such as, Abraham (Judaism), Jesus' disciples (Christianity), Mohammed (Islam), Gautama Buddha (Buddhism), Confucius (Confucianism), Martin Luther (Protestantism), the Wesley brothers (Methodism), Mary Baker Eddy (Christian Science);
  - religious heroes and heroines—including defenders of the faith, martyrs, leaders, reformers, teachers, musicians, builders, missionaries, and scholars;

77

- significant influences in the recent era—such as Mother Theresa in India, Dr. Albert Schweitzer in Africa, and Mahatma Gandhi's life of nonviolent resistance.
- your child's acquaintances—relatives, teachers, neighbors, ministers, priests, rabbis, elders, or gurus.

• *You can put your child in touch with spiritual examples by*

- giving him good books to read, especially biographies and autobiographies;
- using the multimedia that are available—TV, computer communication, videos, drama, and theater;
- taking him to places of worship;
- choosing schools where spiritual development is recognized;
- enrolling him in out-of-school study groups and recreation groups where spiritual values are nurtured.

• *Put your child in touch with role models that are a little further along than she is.*

Children will naturally look up to and learn from somebody who is a little older than they are. For instance, a preschooler may enjoy hearing the stories about a child of early school age; a school-age child about an adolescent who made a faith commitment; a pre-adolescent about a teenager who wrestled with questions of his calling or vocation.

Let their accounts answer questions that are forming in your child's mind, or show the possibilities and adventures in the life of faith that he can appreciate:

- episodes of obedience, doing good, and straightforward decision making will likely appeal to *preschoolers*;
- daring-do, action, and thrills will interest *six to ten year olds*;

- *pre-adolescents* will probably respond best to high moral choices and adventures far afield;
- *teenagers* may be ready to learn of personal and psychological risk taking, character flaws, inner conflicts, self-doubts, and their resolutions.

Introducing a child to spiritual examples a little beyond his own level of development avoids talking down to him—he will not respond well to being treated as a "baby," as he will be quick to tell you. By exposing him to the next "step" in his spiritual journey, you can draw him forward into more mature ways of thinking about and acting out his faith.

20

~~~~~~

LEARNING THROUGH PARENTS

Parents can influence a child's understanding of God more than anyone else.

The first and probably the most enduring picture children develop of God is the picture they have of their parents. Psychoanalyst Ana-Maria Rizzuto, in her book *The Birth of the Living God*, demonstrates that if a child sees her mother and father as predictably trustworthy, kind, and approachable, there is a strong likelihood that she will also see God as predictably trustworthy, kind, and approachable. It is equally likely that if a child sees her parents as harsh, indifferent, or unfair, then she will regard God as harsh, indifferent, or unfair. ***Parents can influence a child's understanding of God more than anyone else.***

Sally Pierson Dillon, a Christian woman, tells this story about her father.

> For her tenth birthday, the whole family went to the beach. While Mom and her sisters sprawled on the sand, she and Dad went off to explore the rock pools, where they found a baby octopus.
> Sally was told to wait by the pool while Dad went back to get the rest of the family to come see their find. His parting words were, "If the octopus tries to get away, let it go. Do not touch it. OK?"
> Watching Dad's figure grow smaller in the distance, Sally thought about how smooth and soft the octopus looked. She poked out one finger and stroked its little

head. Nothing bad happened, so she stroked him again with her palm.

A long tentacle came up out of the water and stroked the back of her hand. "He likes me," she thought.

Then the tentacle wrapped around her arm, tightly. She reached in with her other hand to untangle him, when another tentacle came out of the water and wrapped around that arm. She pulled away, but he seemed to be made of taffy—he just stretched with her but did not let go.

She tried pushing him off with her foot, but more tentacles came and wrapped around her leg. "Stupid octopus," she yelled, "Let me go!" and with that she toppled over into the water. Spluttering in the waves, she felt more tentacles catch around her face.

Luckily, the rest of the family was on their way to see the creature and Dad saw Sally's predicament. He pulled her up out of the water but couldn't pull the slippery little creature off, either, so he drew Sally close to him and gradually coaxed those tight tentacles to wrap around his arms and legs. Bit by bit, the octopus transferred to him, where Dad could eventually pluck him off.

On the way home in the car, Sally snuggled close to Dad, feeling bad about the welts that he would carry on his limbs for many months. He didn't reproach her or get angry. He simply rescued her, and she was full of contrition and gratitude.

Whenever she remembers the episode with the octopus, she says, she is reminded of God.

Not all children can recall major moments of insight like this one, but in the daily relationship between parent and child, the child is learning about God. What can you do to make a positive difference in a child's perceptions of God?

Let Your Child Know You Love Him

This seems so obvious that it may hardly warrant saying, but the fact is that many children do not know how much their parents really love them. Consider these simple strategies for communicating this message:

- As you tuck him into bed, greet him in the morning, or say good-bye to him as he leaves for school, say, "I love you."
- Touch him lovingly, give hugs, and sit him on your knee.
- Find time to really listen to him and talk with him; to laugh and play with him; to be sad with him; to face the difficult moments with him; to worship with him.

Be Trustworthy

Although trust is something to be earned, trust in you as a parent is something your child came into the world wanting to give you.

- Keep your promises and only threaten to do what you would be willing to carry out.
- Be predictable. If something is expected of her one day, it should be expected every day. If something is forbidden one moment, it should remain forbidden the next moment—unless you are clear that you have changed your mind for good reason.
- Be consistent. If it is wrong for her to tell a lie, then it is wrong for you to tell a lie. If it is right for you to be angry when thwarted, then it is right for her. If it is good for her to go to services, then it is good for you.
- Be there. When you are needed to support her through a musical performance or a ball game, you are in the audience. When you are needed to help her deal with some unfairness, you take part. When she faces something fearful, you have support and courage to share. When she has done well, you are there to commend. When she has tried and failed, you are there to encourage. When she has done wrong, you are there to reprimand but also to forgive.
- Make your reprimands and punishments fit the wrong— don't let your feelings carry your response to excess.
- Be quick to notice when she does something good. A smile, a thank you, a hug, or a word of praise builds trust, happiness, and self-confidence.

Be Fair

Children have a finely tuned sense of justice. They notice whether you have the same rules for all, to whom you gave the best present, with whom you spent the most time, and who makes you light up the brightest. Do not show favoritism to one over another. If a new baby arrives in your family, do not neglect the older child, but make him part of the larger circle you now have.

21

‸‸

LEARNING EVEN THOUGH PARENTS MAKE MISTAKES

You can represent God in the way you deal with your mistakes.

In a spiritual growth workshop several years ago, a mother and her seven-year-old son, David, set about to draw their pictures of God. When they were done, all the members in the circle shared their drawings and insights. David showed a drawing of a bearded man, slim, athletic, raised up on a high throne above the ground. As he talked about his drawing, his mother gasped. She quickly recognized that David had drawn a picture of God that could just as easily have been of his dad—right down to the beard. The tragedy of the story was that at the time, dad had left the family. David and his mother and older brother were in a great deal of pain over the impending divorce. Would God become someone who would abandon him, too?

Parents who realize the impact of their actions and relationships in the lives and faith of their children may very well feel overwhelmed by the idea that they will be pictures of God for their children. The case studies in Ana-Maria Rizzuto's *The Birth of the Living God* are distressing because all her clients were in need of therapy both in their personal lives and in their religious faith. For some reason or other, the grown children's pictures of God were psychologically destructive because their parents were less than perfect.

But then, who is the perfect parent? Certainly no one any of us knows! But for every distressing case we might read about in the book, we can recall other cases where children do grow up to love and trust God as they love and trust their parents. If no parent is without some faults and flaws, how is this possible? In essence, *you can represent God in the way you deal with your mistakes.* This involves the following key steps.

Recognize and Admit Your Mistakes

In the quiet moments at the end of a day, occasionally take time to reflect on the day's events and activities. When were you with your child? What interactions were there? How do you rate these interactions—were they great, OK, or poor?

For the better moments in your interactions with your child, ask yourself what made them so good? What would you like to remember for next time?

For those disappointing moments with him (every parent has them), try to think how you could have done better and imagine from there how events would have unfolded. If we can imagine a better tomorrow, then maybe it can happen for real.

If you recall a specific moment in the day in which your actions and responses were hurtful or let your child down in some way, admit this to yourself and him at the first opportunity you have. In making things right between you by saying you are sorry and taking steps toward doing better, you can point him beyond your inadequacy to God.

Remember a Picture Does Not Copy, but It Represents

The answer to your worries about your mistakes comes back in part to what it means to be a picture. A picture is not an exact copy but a representation. It captures something of what it portrays, although it can never capture it entirely. It gives an idea, a rough sketch, which makes us think about what it portrays. It points in the right direction. Imagination, faith, belief, and hope fill in the gaps. As representations of God—and this you cannot escape—you can live a life that will point your child Godward, even through the clouds of your own mistakes.

When Moses delivered the Ten Commandments and the many other supplementary decrees, laws, and promises to the people of Israel, he realized the enormous responsibility resting on parents to impart a knowledge of God to future generations. His advice to the Hebrew mothers and fathers was that they impress these things on their children in everything they did. They should talk about them when they were walking, or sitting, or going to bed. They should tie them on their hands and foreheads and write them on their doorframes and gateposts!

It was not as though the parents could do these things literally—there were too many words to fit on most doorframes and gateposts and certainly on foreheads and hands for a start. Life would come to a stop if every moment had to be filled up with telling the laws over and over.

But figuratively, it was possible. These Hebrew parents were being advised to fill their lives and homes with God's words, *as if* they were built into the very structures of the homes and carried about in their very beings. These words were to shape everything they did, even in the ups and downs of their experience. Hindus express a similar idea with their saying, "Keep the name of the Lord spinning in the midst of all your activities."

In all your doings, words, and interactions with your child, you can create an *atmosphere* and a *context* in which God can be discovered. If the *overall* picture is true to the will and purposes of God and if your relationship with your child is *consistently* loving, mistakes are easier to forgive and forget. If you and your child have built love and trust over the course of time, she will be ready to give God love and trust, too.

22

LEARNING THROUGH THE NATURAL WORLD

The natural world is God's other great lesson book.

M any find spiritual inspiration in the natural wonders around them. People of ancient roots have seen God in some stunningly majestic mountain top; a far-spreading, sheltering tree; a strikingly beautiful lake; a deep somber cave; the powerful bear; the swift leopard; and the soaring eagle. Today, many people like to be in the great outdoors where they can experience God more intimately away from the demands of their daily lives.

Even for city dwellers in the big urban centers and concrete jungles of modern society, nature still perseveres in breaking through. We see it in the blossoming trees that line the streets, the birds that build their homes under the eaves, the changing seasons that sweep through neighborhoods, the flower boxes that decorate homes, and even the dandelions that are determined to grow through the cracks in the pavement. We see these things and wonder about God.

In numerous ways, the natural world speaks to us about God. God's *generosity* is seen in the sheer abundance of nature—the prolific number of seeds we find in seed pods, the variety of trees in the woods, the array of colors the common geranium comes in, the massive piles of leaves we rake up each fall, the amount of rain that can fall in an hour, the vastness of the ocean.

The *restoration* God can bring about in our lives is suggested by the re-creation that nature passes through—in the return of spring, the restoration of the landscape after a hurricane, fire, flood, or eruption, the birth of new life, and the migration of birds and animals.

God's *care* is seen in the chickadees that survive the coldest winter, the first faltering steps of the newborn calf under the watch of its mother, and the return of the butterflies after their long flight.

God's *power* is seen in the wonders of the galaxies and the intricacies of the building blocks of life.

God's *love of the beautiful* is seen in the colors and sounds of the woodland, spectacular sunsets, dancing waterfalls, and reflecting pools.

God's *enjoyment in creation* is revealed in the kangaroos that hop, the ostriches that run and don't fly, the giraffes with their long necks, the prairie dogs that perch on the edge of their holes, and the monkeys that cavort in the trees.

God's *care for the smallest details* is apparent as we contemplate our own incredible creation.

If scripture is God's first lesson book, ***the natural world is God's other great lesson book.***

Find Nature Everywhere Around You

Together with your child you can find nature at work in all kinds of places:

- walk around your yard or along your street looking for growing, blossoming, living things;
- find opportunities to go to the park or into a field;
- look up at the night sky or watch a sunset or sunrise;
- visit the zoo or aquarium;
- take a camping trip or hike;

- make a garden or grow plants in pots and window boxes;
- keep pets—even fish are interesting.

Teach Your Child to Really Notice the Natural World

The Bible speaks of people who have ears but hear not and eyes but do not see. Nature is so profuse and so near that we often do not see it or hear it, so preoccupied are we with whatever we are doing. To tune your child into the natural world, try these activities:

- sit quietly in some natural setting and let the impressions sink in;
- look for different colors and hues—red, yellow, blue, orange, or the great variety of greens;
- listen for as many different sounds as you can hear—bird calls, rustling leaves, running water, or crickets chirping;
- search for the homes creatures live in (such as cocoons, nests, holes, webs, and ponds);
- make collections of seeds, leaves, feathers, and shells (don't pick wild flowers, for next season's blooms depend on this year's seeding);
- identify grasses, leaves, birds, and flowers using field guide books;
- keep a record of the birds sighted;
- take a camera or drawing materials to record the beauty of field trips;
- use a telescope, microscope, or magnifying glass to examine things found outdoors;
- go on guided nature walks with a park ranger or other expert.

Make the Connection Between the Natural World and God

This requires a light touch, for nature can largely speak for itself about God. You might, however, on occasion take the opportunity to:

- make a comment such as, "God must love variety," "God is a wonderful designer," "God is tremendously powerful," "God cares for little things," or "God is big."
- ask your child what he thinks about God when he sees a sunset, canyon, forest, waterfall, or persistent sparrows;
- read a passage of scripture that fits the time and occasion—for instance, you could read Psalm 19 from the Bible after you have watched and wondered about the stars, for it describes the heavens declaring the glory of God and the skies proclaiming the work of God's hands.

Use Nature as a Guide for Dealing with Evil

Nature, like humankind, has its dark side. As well as flowers and bird songs and majestic landscapes, there are also predators, natural disasters, and decay. Instead of ignoring these destructive forces:

- illustrate the inevitability of death by observing the life cycle of plants and animals;
- let your child see that death is like rest when the time comes, for the fallen leaves and dead animals lie still and quiet;
- speak about evil as random and senseless as you watch floodwaters rise, see the aftermath of a storm or volcano, or observe the devastation of a forest fire—then your child will not be so ready to blame herself when evil comes to her;
- look for new life that replaces death and decay—new buds, a predator that can feed its babies, compost that turns into rich soil for new growth, and the return of plant and animal life that covers the wounds of a catastrophe.

91

23

~~~~~~

LEARNING THROUGH MUSIC AND MOVEMENT

When words fail, music and movement can help a child learn about God.

I n teaching your child about God in a way that makes the idea personally powerful, you are sometimes at a loss for words. How can you tell her how awesome and wonderful God is, how infinite yet how near God is, and how powerful and yet how good and caring God is? ***When words fail, music and movement can help teach a child about God.***

The music of faith comes in many different varieties. Most of the faith traditions have their own religious music, because music has long been recognized as one of the languages of religion. These music traditions are usually shared with children from a young age. Many families consider it a great privilege when their child is chosen for special preparation as a musician for worship services. Jewish children will chant the blessings before and after the Torah readings, and sometimes the Torah portions according to their assigned cantillation notes as part of their participation in their Bar or Bat Mitzvah services.

Jewish families teach their children Sabbath songs such as "Lecha Dodi" ("Welcome Sabbath Bride") and "Shalom Aleichem" ("Welcome Angels of Sabbath Peace") as well as the music associated with all the holy days of the religious calendar: the joyous songs of Purim (the lighthearted holiday celebrating the deliverance of the Jewish people from Persia as recorded in the Book of Esther); the more serious songs of Rosh Hashanah (the beginning of the new year); the somber music of Yom Kippur (Day of Atonement). During Passover, as families reenact the final night in Egypt when the Hebrews were released from domination, children are brought right into the ritual by music. In many homes, the youngest child sings four questions about what the family is doing and about the meaning of the various symbols employed. These questions are answered as the family reads scripture, retells the story, and performs the ritual.

Christian families often sing grace (the blessing offered at mealtimes), bedtime songs, carols for Christmas ("Away in a Manger," "Silent Night," and "Hark the Herald Angels Sing," for instance) and songs that relate to the Bible lessons being taught ("Dare to be a Daniel," "The Woman at the Well," and "All Things Bright and Beautiful," for example).

Along with music, we must also include dance and expressive movement. If you have been in an audience listening to music where it is easy to move around, say at an outdoor band concert, you have probably noticed how the listeners have not been simply passive. We naturally clap, tap our foot, or even dance when we hear spirited music. Little children, who may have fewer inhibitions than their elders, will invent their own little dances and movements to the music.

Just as there are many different kinds of music, so there are many different kinds of movements. We may perform some structured movement in a group or we may perform in the privacy of our own homes. Some confess that when they are alone they like to put on a record and dance to the music for their own creative enjoyment. Sometimes, expressive movement is performed without music in mime, drama, and play. Some have perfected signing for the hearing impaired as an art form that we all can enjoy and appreciate. Rituals are movements that can be both artful and meaningful in a worship context. Bowing for prayer, kneeling or sitting reverently in a place of worship are all expressive movements.

Here are some activities that use music and movement in learning about God. They are merely a starting point; add to this list using your imagination.

Using Songs and Other Music with Words

When ideas are put to music, we can often remember them better. In times and places when people have not been able to read or write, they have been able to learn through singing—so it is with young children. For older children, more complex ideas and more enjoyable learning experiences can be arranged when accompanied by singing.

- For *preschoolers*, sing songs that teach central ideas in simple tunes—for instance, "Jesus Loves Me" is a Christian favorite; "Shabbat Shalom" is sung in Jewish homes.
- For *young elementary school children*, sing in groups, where different voices represent different characters or events; sing songs with a number of different verses.
- For *older elementary school children*, choose some songs that put the actual scripture to music; begin part singing; sing rounds; learn some songs of other faiths; learn to sing some of the great traditional hymns or other music from memory.
- For *teenagers*, sing music of different types—chants, classics, psalms, and popular music; have them create songs of their own composition or write words to known tunes, as they are able; encourage them to join a chorus, oratorio, or other musical groups.

Combine Music and Movement

When children not only hear the music but feel it, they may want to act out what they feel. There are many ways for this to happen.

- For *preschoolers*, use songs with words that suggest literal movements that can be performed as you sing—for instance, trees swaying, people doing things, the wideness of God's love.
- For *elementary school children*, the expressive movements can be further encouraged by allowing them to move freely with the music. Some group dances or movements may also be possible. This is a good age to join a dance class.
- For *teenagers*, participation in a music and movement ensemble might be appealing. They can also be encouraged to create their own songs and dances or expressive movements.

Music without Words Can Be Very Evocative

Not all music of spirit has to have words because music is a language in its own right. The music that stirs our souls is not always and only religious music but may be the great works from the past and present.

- From a young age, expose your child to some of the best music. We all tend to enjoy and understand what we are most familiar with.
- Choose good music that he can appreciate. In Haydn's *The Seasons* or *Creation*, for instance, he can listen for the various sound effects as the story unfolds.
- Find pieces that are written in different styles, use different instruments, appear in different cultures, and express different emotions.

95

〰〰〰〰〰〰〰〰〰〰〰〰〰〰〰〰〰〰〰〰〰〰〰〰〰〰〰〰〰〰〰〰〰〰〰

Acquaint Your Child with Movements and Rituals that
Express Spiritual Understandings

In understanding ourselves and our lives, we not only use our mental powers but also our physical powers and our emotional energy.

- Within your family, choose rituals to mark special occasions—birthdays, the new year, marriages, deaths, and religious festivals. Prepare for them by talking about the event beforehand and getting everything ready on time. Enact them with attention to detail. Make the occasion significant and appealing by explaining its purpose and involving the whole family.
- Teach your child at a very young age how to perform simple gestures, such as folding hands for prayer and walking reverently in a sacred place.
- Encourage your child's own spontaneous expressions as well. For instance, invite her to choose a song to sing; ask her to show you what God means to her, what she thinks of herself, or what a story tells her—without using words. You could put her in touch with the meaning and feelings of a story by asking her to play the role of a character as you tell it.

24

~~~~~~

LEARNING THROUGH ART AND ARCHITECTURE

The eyes are an avenue to the soul.

S acred places are special because they point to God in some way. The architecture may suggest the grandeur or closeness of God. The place may have historical, traditional, or symbolic significance, such as the Temple in Jerusalem, St. Peter's Square in Rome, the River Ganges, or the cubical temple, the *Ka'ba*, in Mecca.

Sacred places come in a great variety. Some traditions have built huge edifices and decorated them in the grandest of ways. Building a cathedral or temple has at times taken generations of craftspeople and workers. The best of design and stone and precious metals have been brought to the task.

A dedicated site often stands out because it is constructed on a large scale. One of the most famous Islamic mosques, the great mosque of Samarra, has room for a hundred thousand people to pray. Inside the mosques, pools of water, fountains, or basins are available for purification rituals. Floors and niches are spotlessly clean. Walls are often decorated with sacred words, for calligraphy is one of Islam's most beautiful art forms.

Ancient Hindu and Buddhist temples are often stunningly lavish and extravagantly decorated. The layout, the dimensions, and the decorative features of sacred sites are often highly symbolic.

In contrast, some peoples have marked sacred space simply with a ring of stones. Others have arranged a personal space where they can reflect and be at peace—by a stream, in a quiet nook in a garden, or alone by a fireside.

To enter a sacred place, whether it is marked by a particular architecture or suggested by a painting, a sculpture, or some other work of art or nature, is for many to enter the presence of God, *for the eyes are an avenue to the soul.*

Diana Eck, in her book *Encountering God*, recounts an experience she, a Christian, had on entering the Hindu temple at Padmanabhaswamy in southern India. The building is constructed as a series of concentric corridors that the worshipper walks through toward an inner sanctum. The way is lit with oil lamps, and drums beat as the mass of people move through.

At the inner chamber, in the dim light and with the drums beating a crescendo, a door in the center is thrown open and the worshippers catch a glimpse of the long reclining figure of Vishnu. Then a door to the right reveals the upper part of the figure; and the door to the left reveals the feet. The impression is that in the inner chamber is an enormous presence, full of mystery and wonder.

The scene brought to her mind some scripture she had learned as a child. As they stood in awe, the priest brought a lamp from the figure to the people gathered around the doors for a blessing. Arms reached out—hers among them—to touch the flame that came from God. The experience in this sacred place was for her both moving and enlightening.

In thinking about sacred places and other artistic representations of God that might have a spiritual impact on your child, consider the points that follow.

Help Your Child Find his Sacred Place

- Have your child close his eyes. Ask him, Where would you most like to be when you pray to God, read scripture, or think about your life?
- Visit the sacred sites in your town—churches, mosques, temples, and Native American sites. Sit quietly in these places. Explain or have someone explain what the various design and artistic features symbolize.
- Let him know that there is a place that is especially his in your house—a room, a chair, or a table place, for instance. Encourage him to spend some quiet time in his place.

Encourage Your Child to Respect the Sacred Places of Others

- Walk reverently; speak softly if at all; avoid staring at worshippers.
- Merge with worshippers where this is appropriate—in singing, praying, listening, or kneeling.

Expose Your Child to Works of Art

- Scatter artwork around your home—on walls and in books (from the library if necessary). Develop a garden nook. Visit art galleries and museums.
- Talk about them with your child. You might begin a conversation by asking, What is this picture telling us? I wonder why this sculpture stands in the cathedral and not in a museum? Why do so many worship places have tall spires? Why would people put gold in their worship places? Why do the people in this painting look happy (or sad, afraid or courageous)? How do we know this painting is about God, even though God is not shown?

Encourage Your Child to Create Her Own Works of Art

• Supply her with materials. She may prefer crayons, paints, blocks, clay, or cutout figures and shapes.

• To get her started you might need to use some kind of prompt—a story she can illustrate, a question that makes her think, an example of artwork on a particular topic to suggest ideas about how she could present that same topic.

• Tracings, rubbings, coloring in, jigsaw puzzles, and other alternatives may help arouse interest.

Through eyes, ears, hands, and minds, children encounter God. The array of materials that can be used is enormous. Experiment with ideas and methods, not only to add interest and variety to your child's learning experiences but to find what will touch her most deeply and help her think and feel most profoundly about spiritual matters.

25

▲▼

LEARNING THROUGH QUESTIONS

Teaching questions come in many forms.

Teaching is not always telling. Sometimes teaching is asking—and allowing learners to find their own answers. Usually the most life-changing, productive teaching puts the learner at the center of the thinking, the wondering, the experimenting, and the discovering. You are on the margins, so to speak, prompting, supporting, guiding, helping.

When you see your role in these terms, then you value the questions your child might ask—the "learning questions"—and begin to explore the power in the questions you might ask him—the "teaching questions."

As a tool for learning, **teaching questions come in many forms.**

Factual Recall Questions

These are the simplest questions to phrase, although they can be quite demanding of the memory! They are often of the kind: Who? What? When? Where?

"When did God make the animals?"
"What did Buddha discover under the Bo tree?"
"What are the Ten Commandments?"

These are helpful questions to ask when you want to make sure earlier lessons have been learned and the facts have been understood clearly, or when you want to build on previous knowledge. The major learning you hope will occur does not happen in a vacuum but in the accumulation of facts, ideas, and concepts, so these questions serve a useful purpose.

There are other kinds of questions you might ask, however, that can draw your child into deeper understanding.

Application Questions

These questions encourage children to find ways of applying their learning about God to their own lives.

Peter, afraid of monsters under his bed after the lights are turned out, has heard the story of Daniel in the lions' den. His dad might ask, "When Daniel was afraid of the monsters, what did he do?" "What did God do?" "Can God do that for Peter, too?"

Penny has just heard the story of the boy who brought the loaves and fishes to Jesus when the people were hungry and how Jesus took that gift, prayed, and multiplied it many times over so everyone had enough to eat. Her mother might ask, "Would you like to give something to Jesus too?" "What can Penny give?" "What do you think God can do with that gift?"

Evaluation Questions

Assessing the nature of situations and choices is an important part of decision making and forming values. Evaluative questions may call for analysis, comparison, or predicting outcomes.

James is six. The family has been on an outing, shopping, sightseeing, or hiking. On the way home, his parents might use an evaluative question as a conversation opener:

"What did you see/hear/touch/smell/taste today that you want to thank God for?" or "What did you see today that made you think the most about God?" These are questions for the whole family to respond to.

Betty is a teenager. She has been reading a series of biographies written for her age group. As she has read the stories of these famous men and women, she has been making her assessments of their natures and characters. Then her parents may ask, "Who do you think is most like you?" "How did God use them?" "What did God do for them?"

An older child or young teenager may be challenged by a question such as, "What have you learned from this different religion that helps you understand God better?" In this way, you can encourage the young thinker to discover links between different faiths, especially links that make his understanding of God richer and more meaningful.

Reasoning Questions

These questions often begin with "Why . . .?" They can push your child beyond pat answers to search for deeper justifications and causes, including the hidden motives of the human heart or the grander purposes of God. For example:

"Why does God give people commandments and rules?"
"Why were human beings created last?"
"Why are we respectful when we go into other people's holy places?"

Don't just accept a pat response but keep probing until you are both satisfied with the answer or decide you have reached the point of mystery and wonder.

Interpretive Questions

These probe for meanings or clarifications. They have the potential to deepen comprehension and from there to make truth increasingly relevant. For example:

"What does it mean to 'love God with all your heart'?"

"How is God like a good shepherd? a king? a mother hen?"

"How do you feel when you think about Jonah (Esther, Sapphira, Hasan Al-Basri, or. . .)"

"What does God look like? Can you show me?"

Commitment Questions

These questions most clearly call for more than an intellectual answer. They go beyond reason alone to engage the heart as well. There is a time when it is appropriate to encourage your child to express his faith and understanding and what it might mean to him on a personal level. You might consider questions such as:

"Are you glad God made you?"

"What would you like to do for God?"

"Would you like to join the congregation as a member?"

Of all the questions you might ask, this kind is used sparingly so it can be most effective.

Basic Principles for Asking Questions

Thoughtful questions are powerful teaching tools. Like all power tools they need to be handled carefully and artfully. The art of asking such questions consists of a number of simple principles:

- Ask them occasionally to avoid being tiresome.
- Ask them meditatively to provide time and support for a thoughtful response.
- Ask them gently, as though asking them of yourself, for you, too, are a learner.
- Ask them in the full expectation that you will not always hear the answer you would give because you know that your child has his own learning to do and his own ideas to formulate.

- Ask them in ways that encourage your child to give an answer in his own words, for he has his own meanings to make.
- Listen to your child's answers appreciatively, attentively, affirmatively, for your conversations can build trust and respect between you.

Of course, all the questions you ask must be appropriate to the learner's level of comprehension, interests, and life situation. But the challenge for the questioner is to engage the child's thoughtful energies and to encourage growth in faith and understanding.

26

‸‸‸

THE FUNDAMENTALS OF LEARNING ABOUT GOD

Three important fundamentals underlie teaching about God: faith, imagination, and example.

E ven if we have never thought about it before, we know that when a child asks us a question about God or tells us something she has realized about God, together we are dealing with a unique kind of subject. This is no ordinary or insignificant matter. God is unseen but not unknown; far away and above, yet close by; powerful, yet caring; the subject of study of the best minds throughout human history, but within reach of even young minds. Given how special the subject is, *how* we teach is going to have to match *what* we teach.

Three important fundamentals underlie teaching about God: faith, imagination, and example. Here are some important points to remember about each of these three fundamentals.

Things to Consider in Building Faith

Faith Is Not the Opposite of Reason
    To believe in God is not to put the mind on hold— rather, it is mind and heart and sometimes also the body working together to make meaning in one's life. Faith is built on experience and belief, so it is both wise and thoughtful.

Faith Grows with Trust

Trust, like respect, is earned. If you want your child to have faith in God, you will need to be trustworthy yourself so that what you say about God will be trusted.

The faith tradition that nurtures your child's spiritual growth will also have to be trusted to be effective. When a community is divided and conflicts are not addressed and resolved, or when parents are hostile toward other members or leaders within the group and do not participate in positive and constructive ways for the good of all, a child will be suspicious of what is said about faith and God.

Faith Grows with Acquaintance

As a child becomes increasingly aware of God, his faith will grow. Find many ways for him to experience God—in scripture, in nature, in music and art, in worship services, and in personal quiet times.

Faith Has Its Own Reasons

Faith reaches beyond facts with ideas about the God who powerfully supports all things and at the same time is above and beyond all things.

Some of the reasons for belief in God arise in the human heart. Comfort, a sense of justice, joy, hope, awe, wonder, trust, and confidence are emotional responses to the idea of God that build faith. Explore these responses with your child, letting her name what she feels and connecting these feelings with ideas about God.

Things to Consider When Building Imagination

Imagination Is Not Limited to the Imaginary or Make-Believe

Without imagination, scientists, historians, explorers, mathematicians, architects, politicians, and business executives would not be able to perform their tasks. And neither would people of faith.

Imagination allows us to build meaning out of facts and construct our worlds of understanding. In spiritual development, imagination permits us to see and know the invisible God.

Imagination Can Involve Many Senses

One of the wonderful things about human beings is that we all have our own particular abilities and skills. Some people do their best imagining through words. If this is true of your child, tell her stories, explain things to her, read her scripture, have her write creatively, and so on. Most of us have ability with words, so you can spark the imagination by using spoken and written language.

There are other children, however, who also think imaginatively in sound, sight, movement, touch, or smell. In fact, most of us can imagine in many different ways. Expose your child to God and let him respond and express his learning using as many senses as possible.

He can hear bird songs, the music of worship, the quiet in a sacred place. He can smell roses, incense, and candles burning. He can feel the texture of vestments, cool marble floors, and the water that is used symbolically. He can taste ritual foods. He can act out traditional stories, kneel in the presence of God, and dance expressively.

Imagination Is an Active Process

A child's mind is not simply a blank sheet of paper on which you write. Learning is an active process that requires effort and participation by the learner. Even listening can be an engaging and active process.

To engage the imagination in learning about God, invite a response. A child can draw pictures of significant scenes, play act dramatic moments, make models or puppets, keep a journal, create a garden space, write a story, dance and sing, and engage in a host of other creative activities.

Things to Consider with Regard to *Example*

You Are the Most Important Example for Your Child

Most parents are delighted and often also chagrined when they catch their child in a moment that reminds them of themselves. In their early years, children learn a great deal by copying what they have seen their parents do, and they never totally outgrow this influence throughout their lives. Take time, then, to consider your own beliefs about God and establish your own relationship with God, for these will be powerful shapers of how your child will grow in faith.

It is unrealistic to expect that you will be a perfect example of faith, but you can exemplify what *growing* in faith means—having to deal with doubt as well as belief, and times of discouragement as well as hope. Your example will serve your child well if you undertake your own faith journey in its ups and downs thoughtfully, honestly, and sincerely.

Expose Your Child to Strong Examples of the Living Faith of Others

These examples may be found among the members of your faith community, in the stories your faith tradition has preserved, and in written biographies.

Part Three

〰〰〰〰〰〰〰〰〰〰〰〰〰〰〰〰〰〰〰〰〰〰〰〰〰〰〰〰〰〰〰〰

WORKING TOGETHER TO TEACH CHILDREN ABOUT GOD

The home is the child's first school and parents are the child's first teachers. The lessons learned from mom and dad in the early years remain with the child throughout life. As you contemplate your task as teachers of faith with this in mind, you realize how big your responsibility is. It can be overwhelming.

This section examines the role of parents in a wide context. You will discover that you are not entirely alone in the responsibility you have toward your child. Apart from your own extended family, there is a wide network of support for parents.

The first few keys of Part Three describe the growing child. Although every child is an individual, all pass through some general patterns of development and stages of growth. Knowing these stages is useful information as you relate to your child.

From there, subsequent keys look at institutions other than the family—the school and religious organizations in particular. Finally, the child is considered within the context of the larger world—with its possibilities and challenges, its richness, and its needs—and how you and your child are a part of it.

27

~~~~~~

THE STAGES OF FAITH— THE PRESCHOOLER

In the early years of life, the seeds of faith are sown.

When your new baby is put in your arms for the very first time, it is a moment like no other. You feel the wonder of a new life. Here is a living, breathing, growing, brand new human being. You are thankful that this little one is alive. You sense the creative power of God.

You are immediately attached to this new life. Nothing in the world will tear you apart. You know that you will protect, cherish, and nurture this baby. This little person has a safe place in your heart and home.

A baby brings hope. Humankind has a future that will be realized in this new life. You are planning to do all in your power to be the kind of parent whose child will grow into a productive, honorable, and successful adult.

In the midst of your deep joy, there may also be some niggling anxieties. Is your child healthy and whole? Are you up to raising this child in today's world? Will you be able to cope with all the exhaustion and worry of bringing up this child? Will this child learn to love and serve God and find meaning in life?

An infant is also a mystery. Who is she? What is going on behind her big baby eyes? What does she feel and know and think?

By the time your little one is ready for school, an amazing number of changes have happened in her life. What might you expect? One thing we know for sure is that *in the early years of life, the seeds of faith are sown.*

Keeping in mind that every child is unique and will follow his own developmental path, here are some patterns in growing faith that often occur in children up until about age five.

The First Images of God are Influenced by the Child's Experience of Mom and Dad

A human baby is one of the most dependent creatures. At first, it cannot feed itself, change itself, or care for its other needs without help. Is someone there when she is hungry? Does someone make her comfortable when she is wet or tired or miserable? Is there a smiling face and warm hugs when she wakes up? Is she handled gently and lovingly? Can she come to you when she is afraid or alone? By learning to trust you, she will learn to trust God.

Ongoing neglect, anger, controlling behavior, or rough handling teaches a child that others cannot be trusted, that she is not loved or lovable, and that she should be afraid of others. These habits of mind and heart become the foundation for how she regards God.

Young Children Have a Wonderful Imagination for Learning

For children up to about three, and on occasion throughout childhood, reality and fantasy are not differentiated. Scriptural stories and make-believe tales can be very real and personal to him. He may also pretend to be various characters in these stories, because he cannot tell apart what he imagines and what is real. Fantastic stories and characters, in fact, are more real to him than abstract rules and principles. Illustrate the great lessons of life using fantasy and story rather than sermons or lectures. Toys and picture books, cut-out figures, and play dough can be used to represent important stories and ideas. Use your imagination to find ways of showing rather than telling.

Preschoolers Think Best in Concrete Images and Symbols

When thinking and talking about their fears and anxieties, little children often dream about giants and monsters. They may make up images or pictures about good things using angels or fairies or fuzzy pussycats. Share representations of good and evil using an array of characters like these, even some of the scary ones, especially those in scripture. Concrete images of good and evil can guide them into appropriate beliefs and making good choices.

A Child's Images of Good and Evil Can Reflect Faith

In their early years, little ones gain a growing sense of death, sexuality, and guilt, along with trust, hope, and courage. Unfortunately, a great number of products for children—electronic games, TV programs, cartoons, toys, and so on—have concrete representations of good and evil (especially evil) that do not represent faith. You are wise to avoid having your child on a steady diet of stories in which killing and violence are entertainment, attacks are made but no hurt is felt, caring is replaced by winning, and there is no accountability or inevitable consequence for actions.

Preschoolers First Steps in Faith Will Be by Imitation

In the first few years of life, children learn an amazing number of things: how to talk, walk, run, skip, jump, tie shoelaces, get dressed, eat with a fork, build sand castles, not pull the cat's tail, and come when called.

113

What is even more amazing is that they learn all these new things mostly by copying what they see you do. Their eyes and ears soak up what is going on around them. This is how they also learn faith.

By watching mom and dad, the young child will learn how to pray, how to respect scripture and sacred places, how to treat others, what to trust, how to have hope, and how to love what is true, beautiful, and good.

28

THE STAGES
OF FAITH—
THE CHILD

*The child begins to acquire straightforward beliefs
and assumes a wider perspective.*

When your child is ready to go to school, you know that he is beginning a new stage of his development. He will meet children his own age and make new friends. He will be learning from teachers other than his mom and dad, and it won't be long before you discover that you are not the only authority in his life.

As his world enlarges, so does his faith. His spiritual life, which had been centered on himself—his anxieties, needs, comforts, and delights—now begins to encompass a wider world. He can better distinguish himself as an individual within the family, school, and other groups.

His ability to speak, added to his new writing and reading skills, opens up wider vistas to him and gives him the tools to describe and arrange his own experience. Between the ages of five and ten, he will gradually acquire the ability to think more logically and arrange ideas in order.

At this age, *the child begins to develop straightforward beliefs and assumes a wider perspective.* In the development of faith, the following new characteristics begin to emerge and develop.

School Age Children Can Appreciate the Stories, Beliefs, and Observances of Their Faith Group

The child's appreciation of stories is one of the significant steps at this stage. He is able to represent and organize what he believes by weaving the symbols of good and evil he used earlier into stories, dramas, and myths. He can understand simple faith truths and begin to participate in rituals and events with some understanding of what they mean.

At this age, children increasingly demonstrate the ability to tell stories not only about others but also about their own lives. Creative writing and drama can be used to good effect in helping children in this age group explain and extend their spiritual understanding. The most appropriate stories will be quite literal—they will be understood on face value, even those that are made up.

Introduce this age group to religious or spiritual rituals in the home and in the congregation. They will want to participate in them and can do so with some understanding of what they mean. Teach them what the various symbols and actions stand for and how to undertake them in the right way and with the right motives.

They can begin to learn some of the fundamental beliefs of their religious tradition. Workbooks and learning materials are usually available from most congregations and can be used at home.

School Age Children Are Better Able to Take the Perspective of Other People

A newly acquired ability of this age group is to imagine how things must feel from someone else's perspective. That development makes this the best age to learn to respect others and feel empathy for those in distress.

This new ability is often manifested in children's acute sense of fairness. They are finely tuned to when they and others have been treated fairly, honestly, and equally. In their minds, fairness is part of the natural world and is as real and present as trees and cars and rain. To be unfair is to break the code of the universe. This capacity for justice can make a child very self-righteous and rigid, but when coupled with learning to care, it gives him a good foundation for future moral growth.

God is usually seen in terms of fairness, often as a partner in a transaction. "I will do this for God, and then God will do this for me" kind of thinking is not unusual.

God Will Be Understood in Human Terms

While at some level, the child will know that God is greater than anything else in all the universe, she will also think of God in human terms. She may see God as a person with legs and arms who walks about and talks. She may imagine God at home in her own house, with meals, beds, and visitors dropping by. She will likely visualize a God who has various emotional responses according to the happenings in the world—God may be angry or smiling, sad or happy.

These kinds of pictures make God more personal and real. A child can relate more readily to a human-like God.

Many faith traditions have developed images of God that are drawn from ordinary life. Sometimes God is seen as a father, a mother, a brother, a king, or a judge, or God may be spoken of as a lion, a bear, the sun, or some other natural object. Children from five to ten years old have a special appreciation of these images. They will be able to talk about what they reveal about God. They will enjoy finishing sentences that begin:

117

If God is our father, then. . .;
God is like a lion because. . .;
I think God is the wind, because. . .

These images also become the object for spiritual devotion and prayer.

For This Age Group, Belief Is Quite Literal

While children can arrange their lives and the world around them in narratives, these stories are usually quite literal. When you tell them that God is our parent, they will take that to mean that God is very much like mom and dad, with the same strengths and possibly limitations as their earthly parents. In other words, beliefs to them are not for reflecting on, but simply for believing in a straightforward way.

Although these concepts may be simple and conventional, this is a good age for laying a firm foundation of them. The ideas about themselves, the world, and God that they gather now will be the very basis for later spiritual reflection. The time will come when they will think through them for deeper conceptual meanings.

29

THE STAGES OF FAITH—THE YOUNG ADOLESCENT

The child moving into adolescence begins to make life-long decisions.

Moving toward and into the teen years is again a time of significant change for the growing child. Her knowledge of the world has expanded considerably through her elementary years. Her reasoning skills now include abstract thinking capabilities. She is stronger, taller, and although many preadolescents will go through an awkward gangly stage, she can do many more things than she could before. Her games are different and her interests begin to change. She is beginning to want to be known as something other than a child.

The years between ten and 14 mark the transition from being a dependent child to being a less dependent young person. Her perception of herself is often forward looking so that she may assume she is more grown-up than she really is. Nevertheless, she may sometimes behave in a much more immature way than you would expect. This is a time of transition, and sometimes she will confuse where she is headed with where she has been. Parents may expect some stormy episodes during these years as this conflict is worked out over time.

Personal development happens on two major fronts during this period. First, the child begins to form a sense of her own identity. Where the five year old moves into the realization that she is an *individual* within the group, the 12 year old begins to discover *who* that individual is. Second, she begins to see herself and the world around her as interrelated. She wants to know and be known by others.

During the tumultuous years of preadolescence into adolescence, *the growing child begins to make lifelong decisions.* These will reflect her faith and help set its course for the future.

The Adolescent Forms a Number of Important Relationships Outside of the Family

Increasingly, school, clubs, church or temple, sport teams, and best friends are the center of interest for adolescents. They have more appointments to keep, more responsibilities to fulfill, and more events to participate in. Many parents feel that their children become strangers to them during these years.

While parents should recognize the adolescent's need for outside interests and connections, they should also continue to give them responsibilities and involvements with the whole family. While young people are rising to the challenge of more personal freedom and independence, they also need the security and enduring values of the home as well. Finding the right balance between these two needs is one of the toughest demands on parents.

The task will be made easier if you have built a base of trust over the years and now are willing to listen to your young people. Joint decision making between you and your child can provide support and guidance as well as fulfill the need now for a measure of self-determination.

You cannot always choose which groups a young person will join, but you can expose him to an array of opportunities that you feel most comfortable with. If you belong to a faith tradition, he may find some congenial groups there. Encourage him to join clubs and teams that will provide wholesome activities and give him opportunities to meet other young people with similar interests.

Connections with a group that is not only for fun but also serves some worthy cause, such as Big Brothers/Big Sisters, Girl or Boy Scouts, nature or conservation clubs, can be very appealing to this age group. They are looking for their place in the world and a sense of being needed.

Close Friendships Become Very Important

Adolescents need a best friend—or several best friends—to talk with, scheme with, fantasize with, and share their secrets with. Some researchers have called this the need for a "mirror"—that is, someone who will reflect them as they endeavor to discover who they are.

This mutual need for "mirrors" manifests itself in a number of ways. This age group will develop almost oppressive codes about what to wear, how to style their hair, how to talk, and even how to walk. Part of their choice is influenced by the need to assert themselves as different from their parents; part by the need to be the same as everybody else. Such is the confusion of adolescence.

The practice of forming close friends is an early step toward finding a group of lifelong best friends and, eventually, a marriage partner.

Adolescence Is a Period of Conformity and Convention

Just as adolescents develop particular dress and behavior codes, so they are prone to conform to other conventions within their group. In the insecurity of coming to terms with

121

their own identity, they do not usually want to stand out. If they are taller than their friends, they will often slump; if their friends don't join the choir, they probably will not; if skateboards are in, they must have a skateboard, too.

This pressure to conform also appears in faith groups. Many young people in a peer group choose to be initiated into their tradition at the same time, whether by bar/bat mitzvah, baptism, confirmation, or whatever service the particular tradition has. Parents and youth leaders may be concerned that peer pressure is at work here. A trusted adult should talk with the candidates individually to ascertain that each one is sure he or she wants to take this step.

Do not be surprised to find, however, that your young person genuinely wants to officially claim membership in the faith community during these years. Because this is the age for living by convention, whether developed by peers or some larger group, following the convention of the initiation service and joining a religious group can be the adolescent's way of expressing faith and commitment.

30

~~~~~~

THE CRISES OF FAITH

Faith develops as a series of turning points.

You know that your child goes through a number of growth spurts. One day he has a closet of clothes that fit; the next, you can't keep up with his changes in height and shoe size. Children seem to grow taller and bigger in fits and starts. Growing up is more like climbing a set of uneven stairs than walking up a steady incline. This can be very trying at times for both child and parent, but also very natural and normal.

Just as physical development has its growth spurts, so, too, does spiritual development. ***Faith develops as a series of turning points.*** For some children, these points can be traversed quite smoothly, while for others, it is a time of tension and conflict.

In faith development, some of these turning points are internal, others external. Internally, changes may have been taking place but did not show themselves. It is as though the body or mind or soul consolidates its level of development while quietly gathering energy, then suddenly takes another leap forward toward maturity.

Some of the changes that growing faith depends on are physical. As the body gets bigger and stronger, more skills are learned and more experiences are encountered. These become the bases for new experiences with God and faith in practice.

The mind also learns to deal with knowledge in new ways. For instance, each child gradually accumulates her own fund of memories to call on and develops a number of new abilities as the years pass. An early milestone is being able to imagine objects when they are out of sight. Then she is mentally able to manipulate those objects in new and creative ways. She begins to sort reality from fantasy and feeling from reason. By the time she is an adolescent, she can think more abstractly and logically. She can evaluate and compare and begin to make choices based on reason. Each of these changes gives new quality to faith.

Externally, a number of things can affect faith. A child's social group may help or hinder his spiritual awareness. How his significant others treat him and what kind of regard they show him will influence his picture of God. If the context in which he lives is filled with the good, the true, and the beautiful, he will develop corresponding notions of himself, the world, and others.

Faith is also transformed by memorable experiences. Healthy children suddenly afflicted with a terrible illness or accident will often think about life in new ways. The loss of a loved one, the breakup of a home, moving to a new neighborhood, or other traumatic events have serious effects. Profoundly enjoyable experiences can also do the same, such as a trip down the Grand Canyon, or camping out under the stars, or helping other children in need.

Whatever the turning point may be, it will bring an element of crisis with it. Sometimes the crisis will be as mild as a complaint that he doesn't want to do any more of that "baby stuff" that you had given him for his personal quiet time. At other times, it will distress you to hear him announce something like he doesn't believe in God anymore. Other evidence of crisis will show itself as resistance, rebellion, or noncooperation.

What can you do to support your child through these turning points in faith?

- *Recognize the role of a turning point in your child's personal growth.*
  You cannot protect your child from these crises and changes, nor should you. You cannot avoid them in your own life, either. Rather, recognize them as natural steps toward maturity. Look for them and welcome them.
- *Be patient.*
  During times of change, your child will be helped most if you are patient with him. Scolding him for acting in different ways may do little more than undermine his confidence. Of course, you will want to encourage him to be respectful in expressing his differences and considerate in making requests, but avoid constantly criticizing him. Although he may be in turmoil, you can steady him with your own calmness.
  Patience is enduring. In time, this change period will pass and life will settle down with a new set of norms.
- *Adjust your responses to meet your child's developing perspectives and capabilities.*
  From time to time, you will need to revise your approach to teaching your child about faith. In the earliest years, you will take charge of family worship time, attending services, and providing other activities designed to promote spiritual awareness. As she grows, you will involve her more in the choice and design of these activities. By the time she reaches adolescence, she may want more freedom to choose whether or not to participate with you. For young adults, your role may be little more than advisor—and this only when they invite your input.
- *Allow for some experimentation.*
  With new powers to explore, your child will want to try new approaches. He may surprise you sometimes with his

125

ability to set good goals for himself. Martha designed a Bible reading program for herself that enabled her to read the scripture right through in a year. Kuwesi decided to create a collage of his personal heroes for his bedroom, and his parents were even delighted at some of the choices he made! Kiri set about to learn to play all the hymns and psalms in the songbook. Michael signed up as a junior counselor for summer camp.

Of course, there will be some poor choices, too. If it is feasible, let these choices work themselves out naturally rather than stepping in to prevent them. Your child can learn from his mistakes as well as his successes.

31

PERSONAL QUIET TIME

Provide opportunities for your child to develop the habit of quiet personal time.

In the historic home called "Sunnyside" in Cooranbong, Australia, Ellen White lived with her family and helpers as she established a new Christian college in the town. She was a woman of great faith—that is obvious from her writings and what we know of her work. Part of her secret was that she spent time alone to think about God.

Tucked under the stairs is a little room called The Prayer Room. In it, there is only a comfortable old chair, a lamp and table, a Bible, and some other devotional literature. Any member of the family, could go into the room, close the door, and spend quiet time there to think, to read, and to pray.

Not every home has such a space, but the idea of personal quiet time can work anywhere. It is an important idea because God is so easily crowded out of our minds by the hustle and bustle of everyday living. In quietness and solitude, we can think about the events of our lives, face those things that make us anxious, and let our troubles and fears shrink to their proper proportion. We can evaluate our motives and actions during the past day and plan and imagine a better tomorrow. In this way, we may reduce stress in our lives, live more thoughtfully, and remember God.

Some religious faiths develop highly practiced skills in meditating, but all spiritual growth requires some time for peaceful reflection.

As Taoists say, when water lies still and no wind ruffles it, then one can see reflections in it clearly like in a mirror— right down to the hairs of a man's beard or a woman's eyebrows. Now, if mere water can be clarified when it is still like this, they ask, how much more will the human heart be clarified when it is still? It can reflect heaven and earth and a thousand other things.

As you think about your energetic two or eight or 12 year old, you might despair of ever getting him to sit still and think quietly for more than ten seconds at a time. It is important, however, to *provide opportunities for a child to develop the habit of quiet personal time.*

Children can have their lives consumed with busyness. Apart from school, chores around the house, and friends to play with, children are organized into gym classes, Little League teams, music lessons, scouting trips, parties, school outings, and a host of other activities. Television fills up any gaps in the rest of their waking hours. At the end of the day, very few children have been able to spend a quiet moment with themselves.

Personal quiet time is not a matter of shutting a child away in her room by herself. Some children find this scary. Personal quiet time can be done in the family circle, where everybody is engaged in his or her own activity.

You can help a child learn to make the most of her quiet time by teaching her what to do. Here are some suggestions:

- *Find a regular time and place.*
  Every family has its own schedule. Some families choose five to ten minutes a day; others prefer to turn the TV off for a half hour one evening a week or for the whole evening; and still others find it works best for them and their older children if each family member makes his or her own timetable independently.

The place depends somewhat on what is done during this quiet time. Some activities require a table top, a comfortable chair, a view outdoors, or access to music. Once a regular time and place is chosen, it becomes associated with personal quiet time and this makes it easier to develop the habit of pausing to reflect.

- *Make personal quiet time a family activity.*
  All members of the family need quiet moments to themselves. Parents sometimes think of this as a luxury that they must give up when life is hectic, but they also need this quietude. As your child sees you finding quiet time, teach him to respect your time, as you in turn respect his.

- *Make personal quiet time appropriate for the age and interests of the child.*
  For a restless preschooler, the best you may be able to do is give him some quiet toys to play with—felt cutouts or play dough for telling a story or making a character, a video or audio cassette that he can listen to through headphones, or a picture book to color or look at.

  Once a child is old enough to write, even if at first her sentences are poorly constructed and the spelling is all wrong, keeping a journal is one of the most beneficial reflective activities any age group can engage in. Provide a special book for the purpose. Explain that it is for telling her own story. In it, she can write down her feelings about all the things that happen in her life that are important and worth remembering.

  Encourage an older child to go beyond simply giving a summary of what happened. She should make it a time for reflection by including how these things made her feel, what kinds of questions it made her ask, or what new ideas it suggested to her. Tell her to be honest in writing to herself and assure her that you will never read what she has written unless she invites you to.

Other than keeping a journal, you may encourage your child's thoughtful reflection by providing good books for him to read, art materials for creative activities, music to listen to, or an instrument to compose with.

A child who is old enough and shows a particular interest might be enrolled in a meditation class that teaches him how to sit, how to breathe, and how to let the mind think deeply and freely.

32

^^

FAMILY WORSHIP

A family worshiping together at home can have a life-long impact on a child's spiritual development.

I f you have never considered it before, you might want to think about a regular occasion for spiritual activities within your family circle. Such time together gives you the opportunity to teach your child about God and share with him your values as well as your hopes and disappointments, your questions and answers, your source of strength and your spiritual grounding.

Some families have developed the practice of a *daily* family worship time. Before breakfast or after supper, for instance, they all pause together for worship. Other families prefer a *weekly* worship time, for instance, at the beginning of the Sabbath or on Sunday morning. Still other families have a *yearly* ritual—at the time of Yom Kippur, Christmas, Easter, or Ramadan.

There are also many other occasions that are potentially spiritual, although they often turn out to be just fun days. Of course, these times can be fun, but also consider the possibility for a family prayer of thanks or other worship activity at some appropriate time during the day.

Anniversaries of significant moments in your family history or even the nation can be an occasion for family worship, such as

- wedding anniversaries, when mom and dad first established the family;

- Memorial Day, when we remember those who died for their nation and those whom we have lost from our own family circle through the years;
- Thanksgiving, when we give thanks for our blessings and we share with others.

Events that mark new beginnings are particularly powerful as spiritual celebrations. Here you might consider

- birthdays, which mark the beginning of a new year of life;
- New Year (whether secular, Chinese, or Jewish), which marks the beginning of a new year, a new decade, a new century, or a new age;
- moving into a new house, which begins a new phase of life;
- starting at a new school or a new job;
- establishing a new family configuration, after a death, a marriage, a divorce, the birth of a baby, or the arrival of a newly adopted child;
- beginning a new school term.

Altogether, family time can be for celebrating, teaching, healing, thanksgiving, sharing, or worshiping.

With a little imagination all these events can be times for building faith. *A family worshiping together at home can have a lifelong impact on a child's spiritual development.* It makes the home a more special place—even a sacred place—in the memory throughout life. To make this a reality, here are some guiding principles for conducting family worship.

- *Keep the worship time brief enough to hold your child's interest.*
  It is not the length of the time spent together but the quality of that time that is memorable. Five minutes may be all that is needed, although some families enjoy a much longer time.

- *Include a variety of activities to suit the ages of all involved.*

  Many family worship practices have a prepared format and set activities or traditions that they follow. For some, however, there is much more choice and more responsibility resting on parents.

  When you design the occasion yourselves, you can use the time in a number of different ways. It can be for
  - teaching a religious truth or working through the lessons in a catechism;
  - memorizing a passage of scripture;
  - reading together a passage of scripture or other inspirational or devotional writing;
  - sharing the blessings, disappointments, worries, or joys of the day;
  - praying;
  - singing and learning new songs;
  - sometimes making things right when there has been a falling out in the family.

  You might also want to include something for your own spiritual nurturing, such as reading a passage of scripture or singing a hymn that your child can learn with you.

  If you plan your worship times, you will accomplish more during them. Some families systematically read scripture so that after several years they will have read them through completely. Others plan to learn a new song each week, memorize an important scripture passage each month, or complete a family project such as making a collection of favorite verses to be displayed.

- *Get everyone involved.*

  Many adult children do not remember family worship times fondly. All they recall is that they were made to sit still and quiet while their parents went through some program that they found boring and irrelevant. Worship in the family is an activity for everyone. Find some part for each member to play, whether it is choosing the song, offering the prayer, or reading out loud.

Even the very youngest members of your family should not be left out—bring the baby into the family circle, for God blesses all.

Maintain Some Ritual Elements in the Worship Time

Although you will make sure there is variety and shared participation in your worship together, as a family you might also want to develop some traditions or rituals that are always associated with this time. It may be as simple as where you each sit or what role each family member plays.

Rituals may also be more formal. In welcoming Sabbath, for instance, the mother in a Jewish family lights the Sabbath candles and recites the blessings over the wine and challah (bread). At Hannukah, the story is retold of the restoration of the temple by the Maccabees after its desecration by the Greek king, Antiochus Epiphanes, when a small amount of unpolluted lamp oil, enough for one night, by some miracle actually lasted eight nights. On each night of this season, a candle is lit in memory of the event until all nine candles burn brightly (a candle for each night and a worker candle from which they are originally lit). Tokens and gifts often are shared at each candle lighting. Fried foods such as potato latkes (pancakes) with applesauce or sugar, or jelly donuts are eaten, songs are sung, and games are played with a special dreidel (spinning top).

Christians have home rituals celebrating Christmas, Easter, and other commemorative days. Christmas trees are decorated, gifts are exchanged, and lights are strung about the home. Carol singing, seasonal colors, flowering poinsettias, and special foods (Christmas cookies decorated with red and green, eggnog, roast turkey and cranberry sauce, for instance) become part of the season, to recall the birth of Jesus. At Easter, many homes are decorated with lilies (a symbol of death and resurrection) and the soft pastels of spring become the colors of choice. In the forty days leading up to Easter, many Christians observe Lent, a time for sacrifice and fasting when they give up something they otherwise enjoy. One of the purposes of Lent is to draw the mind toward the sacrifice of Jesus.

Muslims observe Ramadan, a month-long fast period observed from dawn till sunset. This form of worship focuses the mind on spiritual concerns and on the plight of the poor. At the end of the month, Muslim families enjoy a three-day festival of fast breaking, Eid Al-Fitr or Sekerbayram. This festival celebrates the completion of the fast through the help and mercy of God. Families visit one another to share desserts and other sweets. Muslim families may also participate in local, national, or even international competitions for reciting the Koran. These are festive occasions for all ages and can begin with practice runs in the home.

Even when religious rituals are not observed in the home, other rituals can celebrate and develop spiritual values. You might design special foods, activities, music, decorations, costumes, or stories around particular occasions. For birthdays, some families serve the birthday person's favorite dish on a special birthday plate; for the first day of winter, the bird feeder is hung outdoors; the first day of summer, the family takes a picnic supper to a nearby park; on the first weekend in spring, they all wear some new item of clothing to celebrate new beginnings; on Memorial Day, they all carry flowers to the cemetery; on New Year's Day, they write out their resolutions and wishes for the new year, seal them, and string them along a mantel or around a tree; at

Thanksgiving, they make a table centerpiece in fall colors and objects from the garden; at the beginning of a new decade they assemble a time capsule of memories and precious things and bury it in the yard until some specified future date.

Rituals such as these and others that you develop yourself can become times for reflection and anchors, long to be remembered.

33

^^

ATTENDING SERVICES

Becoming part of a religious community can sustain faith for a lifetime.

Religious communities develop organizations to maintain themselves, build sacred places to meet in, develop theologies to express their faith, gather traditions over the centuries, and design processes for admitting new members. On the surface, they may look like other organizations and clubs, but religious communities exist to teach people about God and connect them with God.

The family that has found a community that nurtures its faith has a wonderful resource to help them teach their children about God. ***Becoming part of a religious community can sustain faith for a lifetime.***

If you are looking for a community to join, seek out one that not only speaks about faith in ways that you find helpful, but one that also builds the faith of every member of the family. If you have already found a community that satisfies you, work with them to develop programs for all age groups.

What Parents Can Do

Bring Your Child to Services, Don't Send Her

If attending services is important in the spiritual life, then it is important for every one to attend. Show your child how you regard the service time and how to participate in it.

Encourage Your Child to Participate as a Member of the Congregation

Have your child meet the staff, join in the children's activities, take part in the preparatory classes for initiation into membership, and attend services regularly. Most congregations will have a variety of offerings for him.

Teach Your Child How to Behave in a Sacred Place

If you have ever attended services with a restless two year old, you know something of this challenge—especially if the service requires the congregation to be quiet and still for a significant length of time. An hour in the life of an adult is like an eternity in the life of a healthy, active child. Not only do some children distract their parents, but some embarrass them by disrupting others.

There is no magic formula for keeping your child quiet during service time. Some children are by nature more active and more difficult to manage in these circumstances than other children. Whatever the personality of your child, keep in mind that the object of the exercise is not just to sit still and be quiet but to worship and learn about God. To this end, you might try the following:

- Prepare your child for the service by explaining to him in simple language where you are going and why.
  You might say, "Tomorrow we are going to put on our nice clothes. And we are going in the car somewhere very special. We are going to God's house. We will hear stories and sing songs. But when we are in God's house, we have to walk quietly and sit still."
- Take your child to the place of service during the week to experience its stillness and talk about its various features and what they mean.
- Develop the habit of reverence by providing occasions during the week for personal quiet time.

If your child has run about unchecked all week, she will hardly know how to sit quietly during the service on the weekend.

- If all else fails, provide your child with some appropriate activity.

Marbles, which can bounce loudly on the floor and roll down the aisles, and toy cars, which run along the seats, are not wise choices! Felt cutouts or toys, picture books (especially on a religious theme) or activity books with a single crayon will probably serve you better. Reserve these particular toys and activities for service time. Put them away during the week so that when they come out again they are special and are associated with the service.

- Choose an appropriate place to sit.

Some parents make sure they sit between their children to forestall any potential disturbances among them. Find a seat that gives you easy access to an exit should one of your children need to go out during the service.

- Simply tell them that leaving their seats during listening time is not appropriate in God's house.

If a child has to go out for any reason, bring him back in as soon as possible.

What You Can Do As a Member of a Religious Community

Help Families with Small Children

Rather than simply complain about a noisy family, you might offer to sit with parents and help by holding the baby, showing a picture book to the restless child, or taking the crying infant outside for a short while. Many houses of worship provide a nursery with a caregiver for children under age three.

Some faiths might provide a ministry for children that reaches beyond the service times. Families in trouble need a caring community. Families that function well can extend their care and concern to other children; they not only help children in difficulty but provide a model of caring for their own child.

Offer a Children's Service

Many larger congregations have staff members to cater for children and young people in a separate service. Nevertheless, there are some advantages to having these children in the adult service for at least part of the time—they are made to feel they belong to the larger congregation and become more accustomed to the program they will one day fully participate in.

Even where a separate service is not always possible, part of the adult service can be reserved for the children. Some invite the children to the front for a story or lesson or they select a children's song to sing. Others give them a role to play during the service, such as carrying banners or candles, singing in the choir, or assisting in a ritual.

Provide a Faith Instruction Class

Most congregations offer classes for their younger members. Sometimes this is called Sunday School or Vacation Bible School. Increasingly, many are coming to realize the benefits of using trained professionals for this task, but you might volunteer to help teach such classes. Printed materials and workbooks, lesson outlines, and teachers' guides are readily available to most faith communities.

34

∀∀∀

CHOOSING A SCHOOL

Choosing the right school can supplement what you teach your child at home.

The first schools were founded by religious organizations to serve religious purposes. They trained religious leaders and preachers and prepared others for service to the religion as choristers or cantors, missionaries, theologians, or scholars. They ensured that the rich tradition of a religion was passed on to the next generation. They taught children to read scripture. Eventually, the secular community came to realize the advantages of educating its citizens and governments began to take more of the responsibility for schooling.

Today, there is a rich assortment of schooling options available to many parents. Public schools are accessible to every child. There are also private schools, both secular and religious. Some of the religious schools are full-time day schools providing religious instruction along with the other subjects in the regular curriculum. Other church operated schools meet outside of regular school hours and offer only religious training. There is also home schooling where the parents are the child's teachers.

Choosing the right school can supplement what you teach your child at home. The school can reinforce the teaching of the home, and enrich and extend it. Sometimes the school may challenge what the home teaches, giving young people the opportunity to defend their beliefs or discover other points of view.

All schools with clear educational goals and a sound educational program have something of value to offer your child. You may have the opportunity to choose a school that you believe best meets the needs of your child.

Here are some of the reasons parents have given for choosing a particular kind of school. They might help you make the right choice of school for your child as well.

Some Reasons for Choosing the Public School

1. I want my child to meet others from a wide variety of backgrounds and faith traditions. That way, he will be more aware of the cultural differences in our community, and hopefully learn how to get along with others. He will find it easier to fit into the community when he leaves school.
2. I want my child to learn how to hold on to her faith, even though those around her do not share all her commitments. I can provide a supportive home base so that she will cope well when she is away from home.
3. I want my child to discover different perspectives so that his own ideas are enriched and extended. At public school he not only will meet children of different cultural and faith groups but will also study about others who are different from him.
4. I know that the public school is part of a large network of schools with an approved syllabus, accredited teachers, and strong supervision.
5. My child can attend religious school out of school hours.
6. I do not have the money needed to pay tuition for private schooling or the time needed for home schooling,

but I believe my child will receive a good basic education at the public school, especially as I cooperate with the teachers and do my part at home.

Some Reasons for Choosing a Religious Day School

1. I want my child to be exposed to teachers who will be the kind of spiritual role models that I endorse.
2. I want my child to be surrounded at school in her formative years by the values and beliefs that are the same as those I accept at home. I want the curriculum, textbook list, reading materials, and subject matter at school to build her faith and not undermine it.
3. I want my child to be exposed to the spiritual dimension in all his classes, where faith and learning are integrated.
4. I want my child to learn those things about her faith tradition that I am not able to teach her at home.
5. I want my child to be trained in how to practice his faith in the way his gifts and talents suggest in choosing a career, in serving his religious tradition, and in his life in the wider community.
6. I want my child to find her friends among those who are of the same faith.
7. I believe the teachers at this school are well trained as well as being truly spiritual. They will give my child a sound education in all his classes.

Some Reasons for Choosing Home Schooling

1. As a parent with a clear understanding of the kind of faith development and the kinds of learning I want for my child, I prefer to supervise her education.
2. I believe young children learn best in the home. I can integrate practical, intellectual, and spiritual development and make the whole learning experience more

natural. I can take him on field trips whenever it seems appropriate to do so. I can call on all the resources of the community if I plan well.

3. I can give my child more individual attention and can better pace her learning according to her ability.

4. I know enough about teaching and I have the state syllabus, curriculum guides, and a wide variety of published materials to guide me through the basic lessons required by law as well as the spiritual lessons I want my child to have.

5. I am able to give my child opportunities for social interaction with children of his own age because a number of home-schoolers meet on a regular basis at the swimming pool, the museum, the gymnasium, the zoo, and the playground. Sometimes, we all teach our children together at somebody's house.

Although these options are described as independent, there is considerable merging among them. If your child is in school, make the home a place of learning, too. A child who is being home-schooled actually learns from a number of different teachers—television, neighbors, educational agencies at community institutions like museums, zoos, and parks, books that are brought into the home, and visitors. Use all this variety to advance your child in faith and knowledge.

35

~~~~~~

CARING FOR GOD'S EARTH

Spirituality is closely associated with how we relate to God's creation.

There are many faith traditions that find the sacred in the living world. A moving example of this is found in the letter written by Chief Seattle to President Washington when the U.S. government was negotiating to buy tribal lands. The chief tells how every part of the earth is sacred to his people—every sandy shore, the mists in the woods, the fields, and the buzzing insects, down to the single pine needle.

In the memories of his people, all nature is holy. To harm the earth, he warned, is to harm its creator. Everything is connected—we each are a strand in the web of life. The rivers are our brothers, the perfumed flowers our sisters, all the bears, the deer, and the great eagles belong to our family.

For a long time, western civilization has treated the earth as something to be exploited. Precious minerals, rain forests, wetlands, streams, and air were there for the taking, and little—if anything—was given back in return. We have come to the point, however, where we are beginning to sense the seriousness of depleted resources, pollution, the extinction of various species of plant and animal life, and man-made disasters. Coming to care for God's good earth is now a matter of survival.

More than that, our relation to God's creation is a spiritual matter. If God brought this world into existence and sustains it, then those who enjoy this creation honor God by caring for it. This includes not trashing our part of the universe, but rather cleaning it up and keeping it clean. We don't gobble up more of its resources than we each need—food, electricity, oil, and other consumer products. We preserve the life of other living creatures on this planet by respecting their habitat. We care for our well-being, too, as creatures of God, and stay away from things that would harm us.

If all creation is able to reveal God, then we learn important lessons from the natural world around us. Spend time in natural settings—parks, gardens, forests, seasides, and mountains.

There is a saying that is as untrue as it is old: "They are so heavenly minded, they are of no earthly good!" The truth is that people who know and trust God, enjoy and respect God's creation and their role in it. This way, they come to know and appreciate God even more. So it is that *spirituality is closely associated with how we relate to God's creation.*

Here are some of the kinds of specific things—and this is just for starters—you and your child can do to care for the earth.

- *Recycle and reuse.*
  Become a part of your community's recycling program, compost vegetable scraps, give used clothes to a local charity, save plastic containers for storing finger paints or toys, and choose environmentally friendly grocery items (such as large containers rather than many small ones, recyclable containers, and unpackaged fruits and vegetables).
  Your child might enjoy collecting the stamps that would otherwise go into the trash, saving the pennies left over

146

from shopping, or building a spaceship out of discarded cartons.

- *Be sparing with what you use.*
  Most of us live in homes with running water, electricity, gas, heat, and cool air. We have access to cars, trains, and buses. All these things are either natural resources or run on natural resources. In your home, you can practice turning off lights and appliances when not in use, keeping the thermostat at comfortable but conservative temperatures, saving water, and walking instead of riding when it's feasible and safe.

- *Shop wisely.*
  Buy good *quality* and buy only the *quantity* that is needed. Consider as junk any items that break quickly or have short appeal. They end up clogging up waste disposal sites, one of our current environmental nightmares.

  Avoid buying more than you or your child needs. When a child's life is crowded with more things than she could possibly use or need, she is apt to be less sensitive to the needs of others or her own spiritual needs.

- *Identify and avoid the harmful.*
  The average home has enough poison in it to kill the entire family. Pesticides, weed killers, detergents, bleaches, drugs, and other products for care and maintenance are on our shelves. Consider the environmental side effects of chemicals before buying.

  Some beneficial substances may become harmful if abused. Other substances should not be in your home in the first place. Watch your own habits and practices and help sensitize your child to what may threaten health or happiness.

- *Develop a health conscience.*
  Caring for yourself as a creature of God is more than not doing bad things—it is also a matter of doing good things.

147

Emphasize these good things, and the bad things may very well take care of themselves.

Some families draw star charts to keep track of the good things. Healthy habits are listed: drink eight glasses of water; go to bed at the right time; get 30 minutes of exercise; and eat five servings of fruit or vegetables. You might also include a bad habit kicked for the day, such as no candy, no cigarettes, no overeating, and so on. For each healthy habit practiced in the day, a star or check mark is added to the individual's chart. All the members of the family can participate in this, including mom and dad.

You cannot afford to ignore some of the serious health issues that could impinge on your child's life. Drugs, unsafe sex, alcohol and tobacco abuse, and teenage suicide are in every neighborhood. Talk about these openly with your growing child from a young age. Respond to him reasonably and caringly, so he can trust you with his secrets. His best protection against these kinds of dangers is a lifelong habit of looking after his health and a strong, consistent sense that he is loved by you.

36

〰〰〰〰〰〰〰〰〰〰〰〰〰〰〰〰〰〰〰〰〰〰〰〰〰〰〰〰〰〰〰〰

REACHING OUT
TO OTHERS

*True learning about God develops into loving God and
in turn loving all that God loves.*

Most faith traditions have a version of what is known as the Golden Rule. A story from the Talmud tells of a nonbeliever who came to Rabbi Hillel with a question and a challenge: "Tell me what Judaism is while standing on one foot!" The rabbi could do that. His reply simply was, "That which you do not like, do not do unto others."

One of the Five Pillars of Islam is the alms tax. Muslims have the duty to give a portion of their income for the poor, the needy, for those whose faith is in need of strengthening, for slaves who want to buy their freedom, for people who have made themselves poor by giving to good causes, or for other worthy projects such as helping needy travelers or building something useful like a public fountain. In this way the duty of reaching out to others is built into their faith.

Many religions are in essence stories about love. According to the first few chapters of the Bible, for instance, God made a world of loving relationships. Between humankind and the natural world, between man and woman, and between human beings and God there was communion, respect, and mutual appreciation. By the third chapter, however, the love story had gone awry. Rebellion, shame, blame, pain, and fear threatened all the bonds of love.

But this is not the last chapter of the Bible. In all the succeeding books, chapters, and verses, the story unfolds of how God works to restore the lost loves. Forgiveness, rescue, restitution, reconciliation—these are the central themes of the history of humanity in relation with God.

True learning about God develops into loving God and in turn loving all that God loves. This is the backdrop against which all our teaching about God unfolds. How can you put that big idea into practice? Here are some suggestions.

Picture God in Relationship to Us

When we think about it, all that we know of God has to do with God's relationship to people. God is the creative force who gave human beings life, rescued people from danger, appeared in dreams, sent teachers, and plans a future home for the faithful.

When you teach that God is the good shepherd, a child sees herself as a sheep; as mother hen, she is the protected chick; as king, she is a loyal subject.

There are some surprises in discovering who God befriends. God's chosen people, the Hebrews, were often fickle, sometimes complaining and hateful, and even running off after false gods. Chosen kings, prophets, and priests could turn against God. Jesus had friends among the rich and famous, but he also reached out to a despised Samaritan woman, Zaccheus, a hated tax collector, a woman guilty of adultery, blind beggars, frightening lepers, self-righteous religious leaders, and even a thief on a cross.

God reaches across cultural barriers, social classes, genders, and racial groups. The power of these pictures, shared simply and directly with your child, will have an impact on how he will regard others, too.

Demonstrate by Precept and *Example*

Not only by telling stories can you make God's all-inclusive mercy and justice real. Every day, you expose your child to your attitudes about yourself, each other, and those beyond your immediate family. What kind of judgmental comments do you make, jokes do you tell, friendships do you form, or caring do you show to others? Whatever your attitude—inclusive and loving or exclusive and belittling—it will be absorbed by your child.

Involve Your Child in Reaching Out to Others

In our needy world, opportunities for reaching out to others are not hard to find. All a family needs is a sympathetic heart, some imagination, and sometimes a little courage and organization.

Together you might volunteer for a shift at the soup kitchen or homeless shelter, distribute food, dress up as clowns for the children's hospital, form a singing band for a retirement home, collect donations for a worthy cause, give to a coat or toy drive—the possibilities are endless.

The story of eight-year-old Jessica appeared on the front page of a local newspaper. When her birthday came along, she chose to give her best present, a doll all dressed up in fashion clothes, to the children's care collection. She wanted to make a contribution and did so with sincerity and some sacrifice. When reporters asked her why she did it, she simply explained, "I wanted to share my things with other children because some of them don't have very much."

Teach Your Child to Give and *to Receive Graciously*

Elijah the prophet stood up bravely for God before a whole nation, but when the drought came he sought food and shelter from the widow of Zarephath. Jesus, who gave his life for the people, nevertheless reached out to others for cool water to drink, a place to rest, and a friend to watch and pray with him.

So you can teach your child that bonds of loving care are formed when we are willing both to give and to receive. If all your reaching out to others is in the form of giving to those considered less fortunate, you may unwittingly teach your child to be self-righteous.

To be interested listeners is to learn from others. To accept graciously the help offered by another is to enhance a sense of mutuality among ourselves. To respect another's choices of religion, lifestyle, career, schooling, and so on is to contribute to a nurturing community for all. And to enjoy the friendship of people of different faiths, ages, ethnic origins, and neighborhoods is to deepen our comprehension of the *family* of God.

37

LEARNING ABOUT
OTHER FAITHS

Learning about the faith of others can strengthen and enrich a child's own faith.

Throughout time and in most cultures, people have developed a form of religion. There are major world religions that are monotheistic—that is, they believe in one God. Judaism, Christianity, and Islam are the main ones. Other religions are polytheistic—that is, they worship God in many forms. Among them are Hinduism and Shintoism. Taoism and Buddhism focus on the processes of being and becoming. Some faiths are naturalistic, drawing meaning and inspiration from the natural world. Among these are the beliefs of Native Americans, many Polynesians, some African groups, and Australian aborigines.

There are a number of good reasons why young people growing up today should learn about the faith of others. One reason is that we need to learn to get along with people who are different from us. We now live in a world where the religions know no boundaries. People of faith have moved to new homes all over the world and most of our communities today are a mix of different beliefs. Your child will meet children of other faiths at school, in the playground, around the neighborhood, and eventually in the workplace.

Religious differences are one of the most divisive forces in society because each religion tends to believe it is right and everybody else is wrong. Also, because religious concepts shape many other things a person believes or does, in religious beliefs we find some of the deepest roots of difference and conflict between people. Sometimes, people have isolated and criticized others of a different faith; at other times, hostility has become open warfare; at worst, people of one faith have tried to exterminate people of another.

If our communities are to be places of peaceful cooperation and coexistence, our children need to develop the knowledge and skills to be able to get along with others. Much ill will between people is simply a matter of ignorance—one group does not understand what the other group believes and does. This can lead to fear and eventually to hostility. Learning about each other can help replace these fears with respect.

Another benefit is that *learning about the faith of others can strengthen and enrich a child's own faith.* Each faith tradition has truths that can help people better understand themselves, the world around them, and God.

From some traditions we have learned to have more respect for the natural world around us; from others we have learned more about what love, obedience, or hope really means. Some can inspire us with their worship rituals while others help us appreciate our own practices more. Some give us new insights into the nature of God. Some can point out to us how materialistic or greedy or oppressive we have been.

To gain real benefits from teaching your child about other faiths, you might consider the following suggestions.

- *Use incidental ways to acquaint your child with other faiths.*
  In everyday life, your child will find evidence of different beliefs. Help him notice these and share with him what they might mean. Together you might

- look for the seasonal greeting cards that are displayed in stores (for instance, Christmas, Hanukkah, New Year, Passover);
- note the holidays and high holy days (such as Ramadan, Yom Kippur, Easter);
- discover the special foods displayed in the international food section in many grocery stores (for instance, kosher foods);
- look for special clothing (such as yarmulkes, prayer shawls, clerical collars, chadors);
- with the permission of worshipers, visit a variety of local sacred sites (such as temples, mosques, cathedrals, Indian burial sites);
- read children's versions of key myths and stories from around the world.

- *Use the resources available in your community.*
  Many resources are produced for multicultural education and may include materials on different faiths. You might check the local children's library, museums, ethnic centers, television and video listings, and children's bookstores.

- *Speak about other faiths with the same respect you would show if one of the believers were there with you.*
  To a believer, her faith is very precious. It makes sense to her, it explains the world to her, and it guides her. Keep this in mind when teaching about another faith. Avoid making fun of the differences, but look for what is helpful.

- *Share what another believes in the context of what you believe.*
  You will not want the new learning to be at cross purposes with what you have been teaching about your own faith. If you have been sharing with your child some concepts about good behavior or who God is or what happens when we die, then you might add some stories or ideas that other people believe about these things.

Together, find how the beliefs may be different, but more important, find how they are similar. This way, your faith is supported and enriched by what others believe. For instance, if you are teaching your child about heaven, you can share descriptions of paradise from another tradition. Description on description will add up to a rich picture of what the afterlife might hold. Hope for the future will be multiplied as these various stories are shared.

Placing these insights in the context of your own faith may help alleviate any fears you have that your child will be tempted to join another faith. It is unlikely that he will convert to another faith, for faith is nurtured in the broad context of your particular family, congregation, and community.

38

~~~~~~

BEING DIFFERENT

Prepare your child for the likelihood that having a particular faith may make him different from others.

Our age has been described as a secular one. To many observers, the majority of people are not as religious as they once seemed to be. Fewer people say they believe in God, and the overall numbers attending services have been going down.

Many of these observations miss the fact that there are also many people looking for a renewed spirituality for themselves and their children. They may not be looking for it in the traditional places and ways and so they are not as easy to identify as being spiritual.

The result is that many children who are developing a personal faith feel very different from those around them. These differences become even more noticeable if your child is the only one wearing a yarmulke to school or saying grace before meals or not eating lunch with everybody else during Ramadan.

Once a child goes to school, he meets others who are different from him. This happens at the same time that he wants to feel he belongs to the group. You will increasingly hear him say, "All the kids are doing it," or "All the kids have one of these," or "Nobody does that." These kinds of forces may pull your child away from the faith practices and beliefs he has learned at home.

At the same time, children growing into young adulthood are also becoming increasingly idealistic. They are looking for rules by which to live. As their circles widen, they seek to find their unique place in the world. If they can find a role for themselves that makes them feel good about who and what they are, they can be very committed to fulfilling that role. These kinds of forces may draw your child closer to the faith you have been sharing with him.

Keeping these different forces in mind, *prepare your child for the likelihood that having a particular faith may make him different from others.*

There is a virtue in being different if it means making a difference in a positive way. Christians tell how Jesus called his handful of disciples "the salt of the earth," meaning that by their different lives they could flavor the whole world.

Explaining the Sense of Being the "Same" and "Different"

You can share with your child a sense that we all are different from everybody else in important ways. Talk with your child about the differences and similarities he finds around him (for instance, between mom and dad, big sister and baby brother, the friend next door and a classmate, a cousin and a story character). You could identify all the big people, then the little people; all the girls, then all the boys; all the brown eyes, then the blue, then the green; all the different kinds of hair; something special that belongs with each person (a car, a toy, a pet, a book, a tool, a smile, or glasses). An older child might identify different beliefs and practices.

Being Glad for Who We Are

Growing children develop a sense of who they are, as distinct from their parents, siblings, and school friends. Treat this awareness in ways that affirm the child, whether those differences are because of special skills the child has, a handicap she manages well, her color or gender, the family income, or the faith she has grown up with.

- *Write a thank-you note to God.*
  Encourage the child to be specific about what she encountered in her day—who she is, the friends she played with, toys she enjoyed, meals she ate, and what she thought about God during the day.
- *Write "My Profile."*
  Prepare a form to be completed that could include items such as: name, age, sex, race, height, weight, eyes, hair, distinguishing marks, special skills and achievements, best friends, hobbies, favorite things, best qualities, and "what I think of God." A comments section might include statements from others, such as parents, siblings, teachers, and spiritual leaders.

Learning to Make Choices

Making decisions is a learned skill. Children whose parents have given them practice in making choices will be better prepared to withstand peer pressure when it might harm them.

Preschoolers

The first choices a child can learn to make will tend to be between two good things. You might ask, "Shall we sing this song or that one for worship tonight?" rather than "Shall we sing a song for worship?" "Which story book will we read from?" rather than "Shall we read a story?"

School Age Children

The choices now could give more options to the child and a greater sense of choosing how she will participate. You might ask, "Who would like to say the prayer?" or "Where would you like to work on your journal?"

Preadolescents

As he considers his own spiritual life, he can begin to make decisions about how to nurture it. You might ask, "Which service would you like to attend?" or "Would you like to organize family worship for us on Tuesdays?"

Preparing a Child for Specific Situations She Might Encounter

As a parent you will probably be able to predict what kinds of pressures your child will face going into a new situation. Help her move into these situations with confidence.

* *Role play.*
  You can practice by role playing. You take the role of somebody who is likely to tease, make fun, or ask questions while your child tries out different responses.
* *Simply talk to her about being different.*
  Let her know that being different is not a bad thing, but in fact something that makes her special. Tell her of your own encounters with feeling different. Assure her that people who are different can make a difference. Although you want to discourage a "holier than thou" attitude, you can speak of faith as a privilege and a gift from God.

39

‸‸‸

APPRECIATING GOOD
AND DEALING
WITH EVIL

*Learning about God is a strong foundation for build-
ing character.*

Teaching children about God is not the same as teaching them right behavior. Religion is not ethics. Faith education is not the same as moral education.

The reason is simple. Faith is much more than morality. Faith is about obedience, but it is also about hope, belief, courage, trust, and love. Put another way, God gives commandments but God also creates, protects, rescues, forgives, strengthens, keeps promises, and saves.

To make all your lessons about God, then, into lessons about doing the right thing is to do only part of the job. A great deal of inspiring and encouraging material is left out. Yet learning about God cannot be separated from learning about good and evil. As children learn to love God, they will want to please God.

Faith traditions picture God as just and merciful, or loving and giving, or caring and trustworthy. God represents the best there is. God is the perfect ideal.

There is an old parable that illustrates how significant having an ideal can be. A long time ago, above a village nestled in a valley, someone had climbed the steep cliffs and laboriously carved a most handsome face in the stone. A story grew up around the carving that one day someone would come to the village who would look just like the face in the rock. That person would be a hero and leader.

One young lad who had heard the story would go out in the early morning and look up admiringly at the face on the rock. He got to know every feature and every detail. He loved that face. It inspired him. He wanted to be as noble as the face that looked down at him.

There came a day when a great danger threatened the village. The people didn't know what to do. The young lad, now grown into a youth, had a solution. The people were glad to follow. Then one wise old woman in the village pointed out that the young man looked exactly like the face in the rock.

By daily looking at the face in the rock, the boy had grown like it.

As you teach with this in mind and as your child responds, *learning about God is a strong foundation for building character.* Then in developing your moral lessons on this foundation, you might find the following suggestions helpful.

Give the Rules for Goodness in Context

Tell the story of how and when God gave rules for people to live by. For instance, when God gave the Ten Commandments, the Hebrew people had just been rescued from slavery in Egypt. They had been brought through amazing adventures to Mt. Sinai. They were about to form their new nation. God reminded them of all this and then gave them the rules that would indicate how they would live as special people. Embedded in this story, the rules become much more than a set of prescriptions—they become a privilege and a sign of loyalty.

Affirm the Good

If you want the good to grow, give it attention. Tell your child, "That was a good choice," or "I saw you do . . . and that made me really proud of you," or "Look at so-and-so doing such a good thing."

If you want to reduce evil, don't give it much attention. Don't watch it on TV, don't point out your child's failings constantly, don't be always disapproving of how people act.

Keep the Rules Few and Simple

Some children grow up with the sense that the scriptures are full of commandments and religion is all about the "don'ts," as in "don't do this" and "don't do that." That is one reason many young people give for leaving their religion.

In fact, the instructions God has given are usually few and simple, whether one looks at the Ten Commandments, Jesus' Sermon on the Mount, the Five Pillars of Islam, or the Eightfold Path of Buddhism.

Treat the Rules According to the Age of the Child
- *For preschoolers:*
  - Express the rules in words they will understand. "Thou shalt not kill" may be better understood as "Do not hurt anyone."
  - Illustrate the rules in stories.
  - Let the story suggest the moral rather than you sermonizing at the end.
- *For the early school years:*
  - Memorize the rules in their simple original form.
  - Encourage the child to tell you in her own words what the moral of a story might be.

- Relate the rules to real life situations your child might be encountering as he widens his circle of relationships.

- *For preadolescents into adolescence:*
  - Explore the wider range of meanings implied by each rule. For instance, your child might be able to see that "Thou shalt not kill" could refer not only to murder, but also to destroying somebody's reputation, hating them in your heart, or not caring for someone when they are in trouble.
  - Explore the conflict that can occur between simple rules. For instance, What should one do when killing someone could save someone else?
  - Talk together about motives for actions. Does the end justify the means? Is somebody who did something wrong for a good reason as guilty as somebody who did it for the wrong reason or who did it without thinking?

Teach What Should Be Done When a Rule Is Broken

Faith is about hope as well as obedience, and hope is needed when things have gone wrong. Find ways of illustrating how to make things right. Walk your child through these steps as they apply to specific instances. This may include:

- admitting and apologizing for the mistake to the person wronged;
- admitting the mistake to God and asking for forgiveness;
- making restitution where appropriate;
- taking steps to avoid the problem again.

Be quick to show that you do not hold a grudge, but put a wrong doing behind you as soon as it has been dealt with.

In all these ways you can open your child to God, who is good.

QUESTIONS AND ANSWERS

How old should a child be before we introduce the idea of God?

Before you can even explain God to your children, you can provide an atmosphere where the presence of God is sensed. When they can understand stories, sing simple songs, and look at picture books, begin to teach them about God.

Do we have to belong to a religion to teach our children about God?

God is not the possession of any particular religion. God is the name given to the ultimate, the most important, and the most holy thing we can imagine. To some, this is a Being they worship. To others, this is the perfect Ideal, the supreme Good. Talk with your child about God whether your idea is a traditional religious one or not.

How shall I answer my child's questions about God if I don't believe in God?

Research suggests that every human being develops an image of God in some form or other, as well as images for evil and fear. If your child's representation of ultimate goodness is a Supreme Being others call God, you should feel free to talk about God in these terms. Such a God is more concrete and real than abstract terms like ultimacy and goodness. Calling

165

the ultimate *God* gives the idea an identity and form children can handle.

Can we teach children to be spiritual without teaching them about God?

Spirituality and religion are not identical, although true religion is also spiritual. Spirituality means being aware of more than the materialistic world. It means valuing and developing the qualities of the human spirit, such as hope, wonder, courage, caring for others, and trust. You can teach spirituality through nature, art, music, literature, relationships with others, and religion. All these ways can be used separately, although used together they can be very powerful.

Learning about God through religion, however, is one of the most effective ways of developing a spiritual life. Here the beliefs are systematic, having been worked out over time. Networks of support are organized with printed materials, lessons, teachers, sacred places, texts, symbols, and rituals. They also offer a community of other believers who share a common faith.

What shall we teach our child if mom and dad belong to different faiths?

There are a number of options for interfaith couples who want their children to have a religious community for their spiritual development. Some choose to raise their children in the faith of both parents. This leaves the ultimate choice for each child to make when she is old enough. It may, however, be both confusing and time-consuming for the growing child, which may predispose her to reject both when she can.

Another alternative is to raise the child in no religion. Although this may reduce the child's confusion over conflicting demands, it may also deprive her of a community and system of beliefs and practices to nurture her faith identity and spiritual development.

Other parents do make the choice between religions, recognizing that it is challenging enough to nurture a child's faith in one tradition. Raising the child in one religion provides her with a single coherent body of beliefs and practices to nurture her faith and makes commitment to a community and belief system more straightforward. In most cases this is the best alternative for parents belonging to different religious traditions, providing that while the child is being raised in one tradition, she learns respect for the other.

In choosing what you shall do, you need to talk things over between yourselves. You may want to consider how important to each of you your faith is, whether you want to share that faith with your child, and what support systems there are for the child in your respective traditions. It is good to have this discussion and come to a decision before you have your child so that your decision is settled without involving her in any conflict or confusion that may arise. When you decide she is old enough to make a wise choice for herself you may gradually lead her into making the final choice.

What could make our child not want to learn about God?

A number of things can turn a child off of learning about God, such as:

> his friends do not belong to the same congregation;
> she has seen too much religious pretense by people who are not sincere about religion;
> he imagines religion is all about prohibitions and commandments and little else;
> she is frightened of God because authorities in her life have been harsh and domineering;

he is self-conscious about participating in religious
   rituals;

God is too far away and too unreal to compete with
   everything else in her life;

God let him down in some way when he asked for help.

Try to discover the root cause of the child's resistance and
work from there to make the learning appealing.

What shall we do if our child is frightened of God?

Religious people respect God and hold God in "holy
fear." That means that they do not treat God flippantly or
carelessly. But reverence and awe can become fear and
fright to a child. Typically parents are concerned if they see
that the child does not like to think about God.

Begin by trying to find out if an authority in the child's
life, such as a teacher, a minister, or even you as parent, has
acted primarily in the role of someone who is always trying
to catch him doing something wrong or as someone who
makes him afraid. Our first images of God grow out of our
strongest impressions of those who are our caretakers when
we are young. If there is a problem here, this is the place to
start making a change.

Compensate for the negative images by providing positive images of God as caring, protecting, saving, keeping
promises, and so on. Associate God with happy times and
good things. Show your child how much you enjoy worship
times, going to services, and learning about God.

GLOSSARY

Awe reverence with fear.

Bhagavad Gita poetic text in honor of the Hindu god Krishna.

Baptism Christian initiation service in which converts are immersed in water or water is sprinkled over them.

Bar mitzvah/bat mitzvah Jewish coming of age of boys at 13 and girls at 12 or 13, when they are old enough to participate in all the Jewish rituals. Usually involves a festive feast with family and friends.

B.C.E. literally, Before the Common Era. Used as a substitute for the term B.C. (*before Christ*), which implies an acceptance of Jesus as Christ.

Bible derived from the Latin word for books. Specifically, the Christian canon of sacred writings. Usually includes the 39 books of the Old Testament and the 27 books of the New Testament.

Buddhism one of the world's major religions, founded by Siddhartha Gautama (566–486 B.C.E.), who became known as the Buddha. Spread through India and much of Asia and more recently to Europe and North America. Among its key teachings are that suffering is a part of existence; that desire is the principal cause of suffering; that by discipline one can overcome desire; and that one is rewarded ultimately with *nirvana*, that is, being absorbed into the supreme spirit.

Catechism a manual of instruction used to teach about Christianity.

C.E. literally, Common Era. Used as a substitute for the term, A.D. (*anno Domini*, in the year of our Lord), which implies an acceptance of Jesus as Christ.

Chador long black veil worn by many Muslim and Hindu women.

Creation the story of the world being made by God.

Christianity the largest of the world's religions. Accepts Jesus Christ as the founder and object of worship, believing he is the *Messiah* promised in Jewish history. Arose in Palestine and the Mediterranean region in the first century C.E. Among its key teachings are that sin alienates human beings from God; that Jesus is both human and divine; that Jesus' life, teachings, and death by crucifixion heal the relationship between God and humankind; and that Jesus offers eternal life to those who accept him.

Christmas a Christian celebration of the birth of Jesus, held each year on December 25. (Some Orthodox Christians celebrate on January 7.)

Church building for public Christian worship.

Commandments ten-point law written by God on tablets of stone and given to Moses on Mt. Sinai. Known also as the Decalogue or "the tablets of covenant."

Confucianism East Asian faith traditions built on the thought of Confucius, known as the First Teacher. Focuses on the ultimate values of human life by asking "What makes life worth living?" and "What virtues and methods of self-discipline will create a worthy human civilization?"

Congregation a community held together by religious bonds.

Crucifixion method of execution involving tying or nailing a person to a cross. The death of Jesus.

Decalogue the Ten Commandments.

Doctrine systematic beliefs of a religious tradition.

Easter Jewish Passover adopted by Christians to commemorate Christ's death and resurrection.

Eightfold Path of Buddhism the path taken to end suffering and the desire that prompts it. Includes right belief; right resolve; right speech; right behavior; right occupation; right effort; right contemplation; right concentration.

Faith a moral or spiritual quality including belief and trust, especially in a higher power. Also, a body of moral, spiritual, or religious truth.

Faith tradition/faith community a group who share a common set of moral, spiritual, or religious truths.

Five Pillars of Islam the five duties of true believers in the Islamic faith are to recite the creed "There is no God but Allah, and Mohammed is his Prophet"; worship one God and pray to him at least three times a day; practice charity and help the needy; fast in the month Ramadan; and make a pilgrimage to Mecca at least once in a lifetime, if possible.

God derived from the Anglo-Saxon word for *good*. The infinite and eternal Being. In less traditional faith systems, may refer to whatever is regarded as the ultimate source of goodness and meaning. Recognized by many religions as the Creator, Sustainer, and Judge of the world. *Monotheism*—belief in one God (including the Christian view of a three-person Godhead of Father, Son, and Holy Spirit). *Polytheism*—belief in many gods. *Atheism*—opposition to belief in God. *Agnosticism*—denying all possibility of knowledge of God.

171

Gospel from the Greek word for *good news*. The announcement and story of the birth, life, and death of Jesus, and the salvation Christians believe this brings. Also, the first four books of the New Testament, which recount Jesus' life.

Guru a Hindu spiritual mentor, teacher, or leader.

Hanukkah or Chanukah. Jewish festival in late December celebrating freedom in memory of a victory in the second century, B.C.E. For eight days, a candle is lit on one of the branches of an eight-branched candlestick. Gifts may be exchanged and special foods are eaten.

Heaven the home of God. A place of beauty, life, worship, and glory.

Hinduism a major world religion, most commonly found in India but with believers throughout the world. Although it has no fixed creed it does have some overall beliefs, including the view that the world has always existed although constantly undergoing transformations or cycles of change; that Brahman is the world-soul or universal essence; that human beings are part of the world-soul and so their souls live forever even though the body may die; and that their duty is to be in harmony with the soul.

Holy consecrated. Sacred. Morally and spiritually perfect. Devoted to God or the worship of God.

Islam a major world religion with roots in Arab lands. Arabic term means *submission* to the one God, Allah. Accepts seventh-century C.E. prophet Muhammad as the last and final messenger of God, so it is the youngest of the major world religions.

Jainism an Indian religion founded in the sixth century B.C.E. Major beliefs are similar to Hinduism and include the ideas that a human being is the product of soul-substance mixed with the consequences of good and bad deeds (karma) in a cycle of rebirths; liberation from the cycle of rebirths is brought about by reducing the bad karma through discipline and knowledge; and no life form should be injured physically, psychologically, or intellectually.

Jihad Islamic command to do good and avoid evil, especially in a struggle against persecution and false belief. May take the form of a holy war.

Judaism a major world religion from which Christianity and Islam later arose. Accepts the Five Books of Moses, *Torah*, as the foundation of God's revelation to humankind. Includes belief in one God; God is Creator and Judge; human beings have free will and must choose between good and evil; justice and truth are primary virtues because God is just and true; the Ten Commandments were given by God as a guide and law for all.

Koran also known as *Qur'an*. The scriptures of Muslims.

Kosher Jewish dietary rules about what should and should not be eaten.

Lent a 40-day period preceding Easter when forms of penance and fasting are undertaken in commemoration of the sacrifice of Jesus.

Meditation contemplation, often in a formal way, especially among Buddhists, Hindus, and Taoists, where it serves to bring tranquility and insight.

Minister preacher or pastor in many Christian churches.

Mosque place of worship for Muslims.

New Testament collection of materials written by early Christians and later canonized as the Christian Bible.

Old Testament Christian name for the books of the Hebrew Bible, which have been adopted as part of the Christian Bible.

Parable a story invented to convey a higher truth.

Paradise home for the blessed after death, often understood as heavenly. May be understood as Eden, the original home of the human family.

Passover Jewish meal and ritual celebrating the rescue of the Hebrews from Egypt when the angel of death "passed over" the homes of believers, protecting them from the death of their firstborn.

Pogrom an organized massacre, especially against Jews.

Priest leader in religious rituals or a religious teacher.

Protestantism Christian religious belief that rose out of controversies and doctrinal differences with the Roman Catholic Church since the beginning of the Reformation in the sixteenth century C.E. There are more than two thousand Protestant groups today.

Purim Jewish holiday commemorating the deliverance of Jews from Persia, as told in the Book of Esther. It is a time for dressing up in costumes, parties, exchanging delicacies, and retelling the Esther story.

Rabbi literally, a teacher. Serves as the intellectual and spiritual leader of the Jewish community.

Ramadan month in which Muslims engage in daytime fast.

Reformation a movement to reform Christian beliefs and practices in the sixteenth and seventeenth centuries, which produced a number of Protestant denominations deeply divided from the Roman Catholic Church.

Reincarnation belief in the rebirth of the soul in successive life forms.

Religion system of beliefs and practices that relate to God or whatever is taken to be ultimate.

Rosh Hashanah the Jewish New Year, a period for introspection and repentance.

Sacred persons, places, or things set apart for their spiritual significance.

Scripture(s) holy books, sacred writings.

Secular concerned with this world, worldly. Not sacred.

Sermon on the Mount a sermon given by Jesus, understood to contain the core of his teaching.

Services religious meetings, usually on a regular basis.

Shintoism a Japanese religion. Beliefs usually include great respect for the natural world and ancestors; royalty can take on divine status; the social group rather than the individual is the important consideration; an emphasis on local cults rather than national religion, so Shintoism is seen in many forms.

Spirituality concerned with the sacred, the holy, and life meanings beyond the surface appearance of the material world.

Talmud collection of explanations and clarifications of the Jewish code.

Taoism a Chinese religion primarily concerned with spiritual transformation of people and societies by freeing people from mundane concerns to live in harmony with deeper, abiding realities. Taoist beliefs emphasize individual, social, and political reintegration with cosmic forces, known as the *Tao*.

Temple building set apart for the presence of God or for worship.

Torah God's revelation to Moses on Mt. Sinai. The five books of Moses or the whole Hebrew scripture.

Transcendence an attribute of God; above and independent of the material world.

Ultimate final, fundamental. Nothing is beyond or greater than.

Vishnu Hindu god believed to be the protector of the universe. Usually depicted in four-armed human form.

Worship reverence and adoration given to God. May be a formal service or an informal devotion.

Yarmulke skullcap traditionally worn by Jewish males in prayer and religious ceremonies to show reverence for God. Orthodox Jews may wear the skullcap all the time. Today, many women also wear a yarmulke.

Yom Kippur Day of Atonement, the most solemn day in the Jewish calendar, when prayers are made for the forgiveness of sins and for a good life for the coming year.

SUGGESTED READING

For Parents

Bennett, William J. *The Book of Virtues: A Treasury of Great Moral Stories.* NY: Simon and Schuster, 1993.

Berg, Elizabeth. *Family Traditions: Celebrations for Holidays and Everyday.* Pleasantville, NY: Reader's Digest, 1992.

Berends, Polly Berrien. *Whole Child/Whole Parent.* NY: Harper and Row, 1983.

_____. *Gently Lead: How to Teach Your Children About God While Finding Out for Yourself.* NY: HarperCollins, 1991.

Coles, Robert. *The Spiritual Life of Children.* Boston: Houghton Mifflin, 1990.

Dargatz, Jan. *Simple Truths: How You Can Teach Your Children the 12 Most Important Lessons in Life.* Nashville, TN: Thomas Nelson, 1995.

Dyer, Wayne W. *What Do You Really Want for Your Children?* NY: Avon Books, 1985.

Eyre, Linda and Richard. *Teaching Your Children Responsibility.* NY: Simon and Schuster, 1982.

_____. *Teaching Your Children Sensitivity.* NY: Simon and Schuster, 1987.

_____. *Teaching Your Children Joy.* NY: Simon and Schuster, 1994.

Fay, Martha. *Children and Religion: Making Choices in a Secular Age* (previously titled *Do Children Need Religion?*). NY: Pantheon Books, 1994.

Fitzpatrick, Jean Grasso. *Something More: Nurturing Your Child's Spiritual Growth.* NY: Viking, 1991.

Ford, Judy. *Wonderful Ways to Love a Child.* Berkeley, CA: Conari Press, 1995.

Fowler, James W. *Stages of Faith: The Psychology of Human Development and the Quest for Meaning.* San Francisco: Harper and Row, 1981.

Gellman, Rabbi Marc and Monsignor Thomas Hartman. *Where Does God Live? Questions and Answers for Parents and Children.* NY: Ballantine, 1992.

Ghezzi, Bert (ed). *Keeping Your Kids Catholic.* Ann Arbor, MI: Servant Publications, 1989.

Habenicht, Donna. *How to Help Your Children Really Love Jesus.* Hagerstown, MD: Review and Herald Publishing Co., 1994.

Hunt, Marvin. *Children's Stories and Object Lessons.* Hagerstown, MD: Review and Herald Publishing Co., 1995.

Hutchinson, Ron. *Five Needs Your Kids Must Have Met at Home.* Grand Rapids, MI: Zondervan, 1995.

Jenkins, Peggy. *Nurturing Spirituality in Children: Simple Hands-on Activities.* Hillsboro, OR: Beyond Words, 1995.

Kushner, Harold S. *When Children Ask About God: A Guide for Parents Who Don't Always Have All the Answers.* NY: Schocken Books, 1971, 1989.

Ladd, Karol. *Parties with a Purpose: Sharing God's Love Through Fantastically Fun Parties.* Nashville, TN: Thomas Nelson, 1993.

Nagel, Greta. *The Tao of Teaching.* NY: Primus Books, 1994.

Rosman, Steven M. *Spiritual Parenting: A Sourcebook for Parents and Teachers*. Wheaton, IL: Theosophical Publishing House, 1994.

Schram, Peninnah. *Jewish Stories One Generation Tells Another*. Northvale, NJ: Jason Aronson, 1993.

Temple, Todd. *52 Simple Ways to Teach Your Children About God*. Nashville, TN: Thomas Nelson Publications, 1991.

Veerman, David R., et al. *101 Questions Children Ask About God—With Answers for Busy Parents*. Wheaton, IL: Tyndale House Publishers, 1992.

_____. *102 Questions Children Ask About the Bible—With Answers for Busy Parents*. Wheaton, IL: Tyndale House Publishers, 1994.

Wolpe, David J. *Teaching Your Children About God: A Modern Jewish Approach*. Salt Lake City, UT: Henry Holt, 1995.

For Children

Beckett, Wendy. *A Child's Book of Prayer in Art*. London: Dorling Kindersley, 1995.

Bennett, William. *The Children's Book of Virtues*. NY: Simon and Schuster, 1995.

Caduto, Michael J. and Joseph Bruchac. *Keepers of the Earth: Native American Stories and Environmental Activities for Children*. Golden, CO: Fulcrum Inc., 1988.

_____. *Keepers of the Animals: Native American Stories and Wildlife Activities for Children*. Golden, CO: Fulcrum Inc., 1991.

_____. *Keepers of Life: Discovering Plants Through Native American Stories and Earth Activities for Children*. Golden, CO: Fulcrum Inc., 1994.

Child, John. *The Rise of Islam.* NY: Peter Bedrick Books, 1992, 1993.

Gellman, Rabbi Marc and Monsignor Thomas Hartman. *How Do You Spell God? Answers to the Big Questions Children Ask from Around the World.* NY: Morrow Junior Books, 1995.

Janoe, Barbara. *Daniel Goes to Meeting.* Terrebonne, OR: Family and Life Enrichment Service, 1988.

Kerdeman, Deborah and Lawrence Kushner. *The Invisible Chariot: An Introduction to Kabbalah and Jewish Spirituality.* Denver, CO: Alternatives in Religious Education, 1986.

L'Engle, Madeleine. *Ladder of Angels: Stories from the Bible. Illustrated by Children of the World.* Scranton, PA: HarperCollins, 1988.

Lewis, Shari. *One-Minute Jewish Stories.* NY: Dell Publications, 1989.

Maxwell, Arthur. *The Bible Story.* 10 volumes. Hagerstown, MD: Review and Herald Publishing Co., 1955, 1975.

Pilling, Ann. *Realms of Gold: Myths and Legends from Around the World.* NY: Kingfisher Books, 1993.

Singer, Isaac Bashevis. *The Power of Light: Eight Stories for Hanukkah.* NY: Sunburst Books, 1980.

Stannard, Russell. *A Short History of God, Me and the Universe.* NY: Random House, 1995.

Taylor, Charron. *Stories to Sleep On: The Beginner's Bible.* NY: Random House, 1995.

INDEX

181

school-age children
  age-appropriate teaching
    materials for, 52
  attention span of, 52
  and faith, 115–118
  making choices, 159
  rules for goodness, 163–164
  sacred writings appropriate
    for, 61
  songs and music for, 94–95
  spiritual role models for, 78
school choices, 141–144
  home schooling, 143–144
  public school, 142–143
  religious day school, 143
Schweitzer, Albert, 78
Seattle, Chief, 145
Sekerbayram, 135
Shiva, 45, 57
shopping wisely, 147
songs, 92–96
spirituality, 34–35
The Spiritual Lives of Children
  (Coles), 11
spiritual models, 76–79
stages of faith
  adolescents/teens, 119–122
  preschoolers, 111–114
  school-age children, 115–118
stories, 20–21, 116
strangers, treatment of, 43–44
suffering, putting in
  perspective, 40–41
Sunday School, 140

Talmud, 149
Taoism, 6, 128

Tao Te Ching, 59
teaching
  aids for, 53–54
  approaches in, 53
  planned, 47
  questions, 101–105
  unplanned, 47–50
teenagers
  and faith, 119–122
  songs and music for, 94–95
  spiritual role models for,
    79
Ten Commandments, 86, 162
timelessness of God, 23–25
Torah, 59, 92
tribute to deceased, 28
Tripitaka, 59
true, 48–50
turning points, 123–126

unplanned learning, 47–50

Vacation Bible School, 140
Van der Leeuw, Gerardus,
  30–31
Vedas, 59
Vishnu, 45, 57, 98

wants vs. needs, 35
weekly worship, 131
Wesley, John and Charles, 77
where did I come from?, 18–21
White, Ellen, 127
wonder, moments of, 32–33

yearly worship, 131
Yom Kippur, 93